SISSY NATION

OTHER BOOKS BY JOHN STRAUSBAUGH

The Drug User: Documents 1840–1960
(coedited with Donald Blaise)

Alone with the President

E: Reflections on the Birth of the Elvis Faith

Rock Til You Drop: The Decline from
Rebellion to Nostalgia

Black Like You: Blackface, Whiteface,
Insult & Imitation in American Popular Culture

SISSY NATION

How America Became a
Culture of Wimps & Stoopits

JOHN STRAUSBAUGH

Fragments of this book originally appeared in the *New York Times*, the *Washington Post*, *New York Press*, and *Cabinet*. Reprinted by permission.

Distributed by Macmillan

FIRST EDITION

Designed by Laura Lindgren

Library of Congress Cataloging-in-Publication Data
Strausbaugh, John.
 Sissy nation : how America became a culture of wimps and stoopits / John Strausbaugh.
  p. cm.
ISBN-13: 978-1-905264-16-2
ISBN-10: 1-905264-16-X
1. United States—Civilization—21st century. 2. National characteristics, American. 3. Political culture—United States. 4. Popular culture—United States. 5. United States—Social conditions—21st century. I. Title.
E169.12.S846 2008
973.92—dc22   2007042782

10 9 8 7 6 5 4 3 2 1

We have now sunk to a depth in which the restatement of the obvious is the first duty of intelligent men.

—George Orwell

America has become Sissy Nation. A culture of fat, soft, stupid, fearful, whiny, infantile, narcissistic, fatalistic, groupthinking victims. Once we were warriors. Now we're just worriers.

Not all Americans are Sissies. But we all swim in the same Sea of Sissiness, and none of us is unaffected by it. Most all of us have some Sissy in us now. We're not the only Sissy Nation on the planet, and in fact, as I'll explain, ultimately our salvation may lie in Sissifying the whole world.

Let's be clear at the start: I don't mean Sissy as in gay versus straight, or girly man versus manly man. The kind of Sissiness I'm talking about is not characterized by a lack of muscles but by a lack of courage and conviction, spine and balls. You may strut around like the biggest, baddest mofo on the block and be a soft and squishy Sissy on the inside. The American Sissy is gay and straight, male and female and whatever, and comes in all shapes, sizes, ethnicities, and faiths.

But yes, we are Sissifying our gay men, too. A couple of generations ago, what self-respecting gay man would rally to the Rainbow Flag? It looks like it was designed by an eight-year-old with a My Little Pony fixation. Jeez, if there was one thing you could always rely on a gay man for it was a sense of style.

And yes, I'm a Sissy. Of course. I'm an American, aren't I?

I'm a Sissy who has watched Sissy Nation develop over my lifetime. I'm a Sissy old enough to have vague memories of how things were before we all became such Sissies. I am now about the age my father was in the 1960s when, as a Republican-leaning

World War II vet, he found himself having to put up with a long-haired, drug-taking, war-protesting son. I hear myself sounding like him sometimes now. Not because I've gone Republican or "conservative," any more than I'm a Democrat or "liberal." Our world is too complex for those kinds of easy, knee-jerk political affiliations now. We need to be more independent in our thinking, more skeptical of all parties. Each of us needs to be a free-thinking party of one, taking each issue at it comes and on its own merits.

No, if I sound cranky and dismayed and fed up with us all, it's not because I've become Ed Anger in my old age. It's because I believe in our potential and am distressed to see us squandering it. I've been around long enough to have watched us retreat from self-exploration to self-indulgence, from the celebration of life to a morbid preoccupation with disease and death, from intellectual curiosity to mental torpor, from rebellious independence to head-bobbing groupthink. I've witnessed our descent into Sissihood, and it really worries me.

If what I write sometimes seems shrill or hurts your feelings, it's because I'm convinced that we often subvert polite speech as a way to avoid speaking about reality. If we've gone so soft and sensitive that we can't even take a joke, then we're really screwed.

We did not Sissify ourselves overnight. It began after World War II, the last war Americans could feel good about, the war that indisputably confirmed the dominance of America's global empire at the same time that the old European empires were crumbling. After that war, we were in a unique position to enjoy some "peace and prosperity," and boy did we. Like the people in a lot of empires before us, we took our position of power as license to grow fat, lazy, and pampered.

Pretty much all of the characteristics of our Sissitude described in this book have been identified from the 1950s on as we manifested them one by one: conformism, groupthink, consumerism, fundamentalism, political correctness, infantile narcissism, manufactured fears and panics, defeatism, laziness, obesity, gender confusion, the cult of victimhood, the flight from reality into virtuality, the mistaking of a lifestyle for a life, and the confusion of a life filled with junk for a fulfilled life.

Sociologists, psychologists, political scientists, preachers, teachers, self-help writers, newspaper commentators, documentary filmmakers, and ranting TV talk-show pundits have warned us about these traits, one after another, as they piled up over the past fifty years. Now things have sunk to a level where we can finally see they're not separate and discrete problems. They are *mutually reinforcing symptoms of one giant Sissy culture* that have come together in a perfect storm of Sissitude. We're not *just* fat, we're not *just* lazy, we're not *just* conformists, we're not *just* narcissists… We're all these things and all the others, rolled up in one big, soft, squishy ball.

So you may have previously been told this or that or another Sissy trait noted in this book, but from the looks of you, you weren't paying much attention. The empire is sagging from its own grotesque weight. We've let ourselves slide to the point where we've got some critical choices to make, *now*. They're more important than whom we're going to elect Sissy in Chief of Sissy Nation this year. We've got to decide whether we want to continue living in a Sissy Nation at all, or instead make a goal-line stand against this trend, and rekindle in ourselves the courage, adventurousness, and self-reliance that built the empire in the first place.

I'd like to think we're not too lazy to try, and not too stupid to figure out how.

But we may be too fearful.

Americans used to be known around the world for their pioneering spirit, their bold individualism, their brashness and ballsiness. We live now in a culture of fear, anxiety, paranoia, and insecurity. We're afraid of everything. We're afraid of sickness, afraid of death, and afraid to really live. We're afraid of sex. We're afraid of food. We're afraid of the air, the water, the soil, the weather. We're afraid that the planet itself is rejecting us.

We're afraid of strangers, outsiders, and "aliens." That they're infecting us with their bombs, their bodies, their beliefs. Not just foreign terrorists but even poor Mexican migrants. They come here to do the work we think is beneath us—mow our lawns, make our beds, watch our kids while we're off doing more important things—but throughout much of the West and Southwest American Sissies are in a hysterical panic about them, as though they were a viral infection (a favorite Sissy metaphor). Before long we'll have completed our own Berlin Wall, our Tex-Mex Maginot Line, to keep them out. God only knows who'll blow our leaves around then.

We're afraid that our neighbors are predators, afraid that our children are sex-crazed, and afraid of ourselves—our own bodies, our minds, our thoughts, our urges. We're afraid of our own individuality. No Sissy is an independent individual, but only a member of an "identity group," usually one that sees itself as somehow victimized or threatened. Individuality itself is suspect. We don't have the courage of our own convictions. We have only the herd mentality.

We're afraid of the real world, of reality itself, so we do whatever we can to ignore it, to insulate ourselves from it, to guard and protect ourselves against it, and to escape from it. We loll in a safely padded, rounded-corners virtual fantasy world, our seat belts tightly secured and our helmets strapped on, fighting virtual fights, having online relationships and sex. We're a lot more familiar and comfortable with this escapist fantasy world and the fantastic creatures that inhabit it—the celebrities and celebutards, MySpace and Facebook friendsters—than with the world outside the bubble. We are quickly transforming our cities—the last zones of wild, unplanned, messy, chaotic human interaction—

into safe, clean, playland replicas where everyone, visitor or resident, is a tourist. If we can we'll expand the bubble until the whole world is a disneyfied virtual version of itself, World World. If a little reality should somehow seep into the bubble—death, disaster, or just simple sadness—we'll medicate.

Our fears and anxieties have infantilized us. Not for nothing do we call our homes "cribs." We've turned our children into Sissies, too. We're so concerned with not bruising their self-esteem that we teach them nothing about self-reliance or self-respect. We supervise and schedulize their every moment. We've medicated them to the eyeballs, too. What kind of behavior is your kid manifesting? Oh yeah, we've got a scrip for that.

Where did all this fear and self-doubt come from? Sometime in the 1970s, the American pioneer spirit simply pooped out. We had our few centuries of westward ho, outward bound, eat my dust, don't tread on my dick, gung-ho can-do adventures. We pushed the envelope as far as we could. Now we're just going to lie down in it for a little nap. You Chinese and Russians and Arab Emirates and all the rest of you go ahead without us. We'll catch up later.

Whole libraries of books and articles have been written about how the 1960s and 1970s taught Americans doubt, distrust, disappointment, and disillusionment. Vietnam, Watergate, assassinations, recession, inflation, the savings and loan collapse, the oil crisis, the Iran hostage crisis, urban decay, urban riots, crime, drugs, the creeping spread of terrorism, the genocide in Biafra, the dragging-on of the Cold War, the petering-out of progressive politics and the bottoming-out of hippie utopianism and the failed promise of the civil rights movement and and and... It all shook our confidence in ourselves, our government, the American experiment, and the whole wide world. By the end of the '70s our collective mood was so dismal that large numbers of Sissies—some disillusioned that the progressive and permissive

'60s and '70s had not led to "the revolution" and utopia, others who had never been comfortable living in progressive and permissive times anyway—went for Ronald Reagan's retro message.

"Forget about the sixties and seventies. They were a mistake. Let's kick it back to the fifties and start over from there."

Reagan was more America's logo than America's leader. It was like one of the Pep Boys was president. He wasn't a for-real president, but he played one on TV, which by then was good enough for us Sissies.

At least he knew how to *act* like a president, something his predecessor Jimmy Carter had found woefully beyond his grasp. Talk about a Sissy. Say what you will about Watergate, Monicagate, or George W. Bush's I'm With Stupid presidency, the Iran hostage crisis was a real low point and watershed of modern presidencies. Carter let a bunch of Iranian college students and a bearded lunatic spank him like their bitch on the global stage. God, how humiliating. President Bottom. Nothing against submissives, but who wants one for president?

In 1979, three years into one of the most inept and dispiriting administrations in modern times, Carter delivered his strange and much-maligned "national malaise" speech. He never actually used the words "national malaise," but he did speak about "a fundamental threat to American democracy." He said:

"The threat is nearly invisible in ordinary ways. It is a crisis of confidence. It is a crisis that strikes at the very heart and soul and spirit of our national will. We can see this crisis in the growing doubt about the meaning of our own lives and in the loss of a unity of purpose for our nation."

This "erosion of our confidence in the future," he went on, "is threatening to destroy the social and the political fabric of America."

Carter was right about this threat. What he forgot to mention was that at least some of it came from our "crisis of confidence" in *him*. Carter's preachily faith-based, passive-aggressive, I-feel-your-pain presidency was both a symptom and a major generator of Sissitude in his time.

In the 1970s it became evident that space really had been the final frontier. Fewer and fewer Americans can remember the space race of the 1960s. Now *that* was a hell of a time to be an American. Or at least a white American male. Those big white hard-ons thrusting up into the sky, spurting their seed into the vast, dark womb of the universe, and inside every seed a white American astronaut curled up like a homunculus. Yeah baby. We were banging the solar system.

It's true that the cosmonauts always looked more manly than we did. Their rockets were longer, fatter. They had a big head at the top and huge balls at the bottom. And when they came back from space cosmonauts didn't float gently down into the sea like sissies. They didn't splash down, they *crashed* down on solid earth like real men.

Still, we beat them to the moon, didn't we. Get back, Ivan, the moon's *our* bitch.

And that's when we lost it. All we'd ever been doing was crossing swords with Ivan.

"Man, space is cold."

"Yeah, and deep too."

When we got to the moon we didn't really know what to do with her, so we just dry-humped her and came home. Knocked a few golf balls around the Sea of Tranquility, saw that it looked pretty much like Arizona, and said, "Gotta go. I'll call ya." Lost her number on the way back to earth. The moon was a giant sand trap, there were no vodka tonics waiting at the nineteenth hole, and we lost interest. That was the end of the American manned space program, right there, the first golf ball on the moon, 1971. A few years later, NASA made it official by announcing that we would not be fertilizing the moon anytime soon, much less heading off to Mars or anywhere else in the solar system. No, we were just going to putter around here at home taking the Space Shuttle in and out of the garage.

The.

Space.

Shuttle.

I knew it was over the first time I read those words. A shuttle bus in space. You don't explore the cosmos in a shuttle bus. Shuttle buses are for trundling handicapped children to physical therapy and senior citizens to the early bird special.

You know who's the real pioneer of manned space flight now? Kazakhstan. That's right. While we were sitting here inside our bubble yukking it up over Borat and his fake Kazakhstan, the real Kazakhstan was selling space rides to American billionaires at $25 million a ticket. There's golf in space again, only now it's entrepreneurial Russian cosmonauts knocking balls into orbit as publicity stunts. They won't say how much they get paid, but I bet you it's more than the $65,000 or so a year astronauts get for peeing in a baggy on the shuttle.

No wonder astronauts go stir crazy and fire up soap opera romances. What the hell else they gonna do piddling around in their shuttle bus for days on end, while the real space jockeys are out playing golf?

But even the Russians aren't exactly blazing a trail for Mars. What should have happened, what would have been best for both sides, was for Ivan to get to the moon first. Oh it woulda been *on*, baby.

"Get off her, Ivan. We saw her first."

"Back off, Yankee. Go fuck Uranus."

The entire surface of the moon would have been paved over with New New Yorks and Laikagrads by 1990, and we'd be on Mars.

We lost interest in exploring the frontier of space because back down here on the ground we got too preoccupied with whining and spitting and carping at one another like kitties in a burlap sack. Nowhere is our Sissitude more evident than in our politics. Our politicians don't offer us many space races anymore. They don't even try to appeal to our courage, our industriousness, our hopes and dreams for the future. They've become just as fearful and fatalistic as the rest of us. They don't have faith in us or themselves any more than we do. Negativity and futility have invaded the way politicians think and inform the way they speak to us. Opposing parties don't offer us alternative paths to a better tomorrow anymore; they present us with alternative threats and ask us to vote according to whatever scares us more—to choose between, say, Global Terrorism or Global Warming. The language of politics has become almost entirely a Sissy language, a language of fear.

Being a nation of Sissy sheep, it makes perfect sense that we have Sissy leaders. I give you George W. Bush. A pampered, draft-dodging, drug-addled Sissy in his youth, incapable of independent thought or action, he came to power in the classic Sissy way: Daddy gave it to him. Give a Sissy power, and what does he become? A bully. A bully is just a Sissy in tough-guy drag. What do bullies do? They lash out at the world around them, destroying and disordering, making others as miserable as they are. I give you George Bush's wars. I mean it in no way as a denigration of America's men and women in uniform when I say that America, as a culture, fights like a Sissy now.

This is not a partisan rant. Left wing, right wing, it's all chicken. George W. Bush is a classic American Sissy who happens to be a Republican and "conservative," but his "liberal" predecessor was also a draft-dodging baby boomer who acted like a Sissy as commander in chief. Clinton's most Sissy act was to look us right in the eye and lie to us about the blowjobs, then drag us all down with him through the impeachment proceedings.

To this day, many liberals insist that the blowjobs demonstrate what a manly and macho man he was. As though a Sissy in power would never coerce a young employee to give him sexual favors at the office. Americans being perpetual adolescents when it comes to sex, both liberals and conservatives failed to understand that the issue wasn't the blowjobs themselves, it was the craven lying about them when he was caught, and the willingness to make the entire nation suffer and pay for his idiotic indiscretions. There was a time when every child in America was taught a parable about another president and a cherry tree, the lesson of which was that a real American hero owns up to his mistakes and transgressions...at least when he's caught. President Buster Cherry must have been absent from school that day.

Americans have become complete Sissies about politics anyway. We speak of "the vast right-wing conspiracy" and "the radical left" as though we actually had either. We don't have a real right or a real left in this country. All we have is Republicrats and Demicans, Middle of the Roadum and Middle of the Roadee. For the past few years no pundit or hack can comment on American presidential politics without mentioning the red state–blue state thing. As though there were two Americas, one deeply conservative and uniformly Republican, the other loony liberal and totally Democrat. Like the Red Sox versus the Yankees. The truth is there is only Sissy Nation, and most states aren't really red or blue; they're muddy, mixed-up, gun-control-and-gay-rights purple.

That's a good thing. Our world today is too complex to be reduced to yes-no left-right red-blue dichotomies. That complexity should free us from knee-jerk party allegiances and idiotic red state–blue state simplicities.

Yet Americans act like the two-party system was created by God on the eighth day and respond to any hint of deviation from his Divine Plan with moral panic. Any candidate who shows the slightest independence or freedom of thought is greeted with horror, even if he's just a crypto-Democrat like Ralph Nader. You'd have thought he was the Antichrist.

American politics has abounded with third-party, fourth-party, niche- and fringe-party candidates. They're often the only ones willing to open public discourse beyond the bland inanities of the major party candidates. Why act like the nation will crumble and our brains will melt if we're presented with more than two (non-)choices?

You'd know some of this if you knew a little history. *But Americans don't study their history. They only "celebrate" their Sistory*—those select bits and pieces of the past that serve them today, usually only as a way to pimp their elitist pretentions or their victimhood, to claim some entitlement they think they're owed or force some respect they haven't earned.

It isn't just history we don't know. Americans are happily ignorant of nearly everything except last night's lottery number and who won the ball game. Among industrialized nations we're below average, and slipping ever lower, in math, science, reading comprehension, and general problem solving. I think you'll agree these are all pretty much essential skills for running an industrialized nation, unless you're going to buy or steal the know-how from others. Which is increasingly what we do. It's true that Americans have never been big on book-learning, and when we were in our nation-building and empire-building stages we got by on sheer guts, cunning, adventurism, and brawn. But we're in a new stage now. The empire was built; the empire builders all died and left it to us, their lazy, pampered, decadent offspring. And in our lazy, pampered, decadent way we're running it into the ground. There's an episode of *Star Trek* where members of a mildly retarded alien race, let's call them the Stoopits, bumble around the galaxies in spaceships they can barely pilot, buying or stealing what they need from smarter species. I've always taken it as a metaphor for us. It won't be long now before America is Planit Stoopit.

Americans were never book-learned, but we weren't lazy, mentally or physically. Now we're both. We've become a nation of Holsteins, fat, lazy, stoopit, and good for nothing but consuming and being consumed. We don't walk a foot, lift a finger, or stir a synapse if we don't have to. And as the decadent inheritors of the American empire, most of the time we *don't* have to. Why walk when you can putz around on a Segway? Why swim when you can ride a Jet Ski? Why climb stairs when you can take the escalator? In New York City, I've gotten on elevators countless times with people who pushed the button for the second floor. *The second floor.* You can't walk one flight of stairs? The Spartans would have speared you on the spot. Elevators shouldn't even be able to stop on the second floor.

Now NASA is talking about building a "space elevator." Why? The astrosissies will only take it to the second floor.

Why keep your body in shape as you age, when there are those little electric carts you can tootle around in? I'm sorry, but I see a lot of people who don't look old or infirm enough to need one of those things. Many of them just look terminally fat and lazy to me. I bet if you stuck a gun to their heads and shouted "Gimme the go-cart, gramps, or I'll blow your brains out!" four out of ten would leap up and run away. Is that mean-spirited of me? Is it "ageist"? Screw that. I'm too old to be ageist. I'm getting old enough that soon my insurance would pay for me to putter around in one of those things if I asked. If it comes to that, I'd rather the insurance company pay for a big, hunky nurse's aide to put the pillow over my face and rid society of my parasitic clinging to life. The Romans would have thrown you a party, drawn you a bath, and handed you the knife.

One of the most obvious signs of our decadent, terminal laziness is our fat. We are among the fattest people on earth (the very fattest being Samoans and other Pacific Islanders, whom we fattened up by getting them to eat as badly as we do). As we spread our decadent American culture around the globe, many other peoples are racing, knock-kneed and wheezing, to match us pound for extra pound, but they've got a long way to go. We are the original Holstein People, and we are freakin' enormous. In New York City, enough of us are still self-absorbed narcissists that Manhattan has not yet—*yet*—sunk under our collective weight. But whenever I get out of New York City and travel around in America, sweet Jesus you're *all* fatties. Does no one in the Midwest own a mirror? I walk around places like Chicago, Cleveland, Kansas City looking like a concentration camp survivor. I'm not little. I'm six-one and 175 pounds. In the Midwest I could be a sideshow exhibit. The Man with the Lowest Body-Mass Index in Four Counties. I could tour the state fairs. I went for a walk one day on Chicago's Navy Pier and there were so many Holstein People lumbering around I was afraid the whole thing was going to crumble into Lake Michigan. Whole families of Holsteins waddled around, grazing nonstop on yard-long hot dogs and buckets-o-fries and dumpster-sized sodas. They ate the way most people breathe, a constant, regular, unconscious inhalation of food. However much bovine growth hormones they're injecting into those "foods," it sure is working. Everyone in the Holstein family is huge. Dad's my height and twice my width and weight, with a head the size of a beachball and a gut I could curl up inside. Mom couldn't get my belt around one thigh. Their calves Junior and Sis, aged maybe ten and eight, are what used to be the size of normal adults. He's already got the kind of gut it used to take decades of dedicated beer drinking to grow, and her knees have already collapsed inward under the load they're bearing, so she wobbles like a Weeble. And this wasn't just one family, or one out of five. I was surrounded by Holsteins. They were everywhere I looked, lumbering slowly around the landscape, grazing, wheezing, blinking their great, sugar-glazed eyes with the same complacent contentedness you see in the eyes of well-fed cows.

Maybe that's the explanation. This was the Midwest, after all. Maybe Americans in the Heartland—the fatty, struggling, infarction-prone Heartland—looked at the faces of their cows, saw the vacant, slow-blinking, cud-chewing contentedness there, and envied them. Hey, how come the cows get to be so fat and stoopit and happy? Why can't we?

It's not only the Midwest, of course. If it were, we could simply build a big corral around the central states and leave them to their cud chewing. We're all getting fat. Everywhere I go around the States I see more and more and more fatties. Not "overweight." Not "plump." Not "junk in the trunk." *FAT. OBESE. YOOGE.* Dad is vast. Mom is ginormous. Junior and Sis are colossal. And studies suggest that Sis's fat is triggering earlier puberty. Girls are hitting puberty now at nine, eight, seven...and counting down. Think about that a second. We're used to hearing about all the social problems of teenage motherhood. Now we have to gear up for preteen mothers. If I revisit the Navy Pier five years from now, will I see an eight-year-old Sis rolling her fat baby down the concourse like a bowling ball? Five years later, will she be a thirteen-year-old grandmother? Eventually we'll be hearing about toddler mothers. Infants having infants. Babies born pregnant. And all of them fat, fat, fat.

When I was in school, there were one or two fat kids in each classroom, and the rest of the kids made merciless fun of them. Now, in many, many classrooms across this great (big, fat) land of ours, there are one or two kids per classroom who *aren't* fat kids.

Why are you doing that to your kids? Really, I'm curious to hear your reason, or at least your excuse.

What, do you find all this "offensive"? Am I being "insensitive"? A fattist? Sorry. You can talk all the polite, politically correct, inoffensively euphemistic talk you want, but fatties are no longer a victimized, misunderstood minority of people with glandular problems and eating disorders. The average American now weighs well above average. Two-thirds of us are overweight. I have seen the fatties, and they are us.

Look, I've been a smoker, on and off, since I was a teenager. I know it's weak and idiotic and it will kill me someday. But I would never shove a pack of smokes into a child's mouth and light them up. And when the day comes they tell me I'm dying of it, if I suddenly start whining that it was all Philip Morris's fault, *please* pry the Zippo from my fingers and light my head on fire.

Why harp on our fat so early in this book, at the risk of provoking at least two-thirds of its potential audience to throw it out a window? Or, more likely, jam it into their mouths and chew it to a pulp?

Because our fat is one of the most obvious, most blatant, and most widespread (literally) signs of our Sissitude. As are all our excuses for it, and all our polite, politically correct, euphemistic ways of talking about it. We love to talk about our fat as though we're helpless victims and all those extra pounds of flesh were somehow forced on us. We're fat because Ronald McDonald rammed those Big Macs down our gullets. We're fat because of corn syrup. We're fat because you told us to quit smoking so we did and don't blame us if we put on weight. We're fat because of our genes. We're fat because of our upbringing.

We're fat, in short, because we're victims of some outside agency, some force beyond our control.

Once we could claim to be fat victims, it naturally became politically incorrect to say that maybe we should be taking some personal responsibility for our fat. That's blaming the victim.

From there, the next logical step was *fat pride*. The real-women-have-curves movement. As though "curves" were what we're talking about here.

You want to see a classic display of how this Sissitude operates?

In July of 2007, as I was writing this, the *New England Journal of Medicine* published a study that said obesity has spread throughout Sissy Nation because the more of us there are who are fat, and the more excuses we come up with for it, the more socially acceptable fat has become. Your chances of getting fat increase, um, hugely if you have fat friends, a fat spouse, fat family members, and so on. Obesity spreads through social networks. (Read the study for yourself—the link to the online version is in the back of this book.)

But, as William Saletan pointed out in *Slate*, that's not what the major media in Sissy Nation said the study said. What the media *reported* this study saying was that obesity is "contagious" (the word appeared in many articles about the study, but nowhere in the study), that it spreads like an "infectious disease" or "virus." In other words, we're not obese because we eat too much and exercise too little and all our friends are fat so we figure what the hey toss me those pork rinds. No, *we're victims of a plague of fat, like victims of cholera or AIDS*. It's not our fault. It's not our responsibility. Where are FEMA and the Centers for Disease Control when we need them? Fat-assed bureaucrats.

I love it when fat women complain that stick-figure fashion models make them feel bad about themselves. That it's just another way the patriarchy demeans women.

I don't know why I have to be the one to tell you this, ladies, but the patriarchs don't run the fashion industry. Gay men and bone-thin older women do. They have what they consider practical reasons for showing you their designs hanging from models built like coat hangers with legs. Complain to them. The patriarchs got nothing to do with it. Most of the straight men out there don't find those concentration-camp teenagers any more appealing than you do.

And anyway, you *should* feel bad about yourself. You're obese. And you've made your kids obese. Your kids will have diabetes by the time Sis hits puberty. You should feel bad. You should be *ashamed* of yourself.

It does make me wonder what we're all being fattened up for. I know you've seen that famous aliens-with-a-cookbook *Twilight Zone*. But it doesn't have to be space aliens. My money's on the Chinese. There are more than a billion of them. They gotta be hungry. They gotta be sick of eating a cup of rice a day. Mmmm, American ham. Comes with its own Krispy Kreme sugar glaze.

Maybe we should invite a delegation of those lean and hungry barbarians to come over here and start cutting the fattest, juiciest Americans from the herd. I bet *that* would get you off the couch and into the gym. I bet you—

Oh, wait. The switchboard is all lit up. Let's take a call. Go ahead, Sissy, you're on the page.

Sissy: "As a person of Asian heritage, I find what you just wrote highly offensive."

Me: What? I'm not saying you eat cats. Cannibalism is a couple rungs up the evolutionary ladder. Shut up and eat your Americans.

Besides, nothing signals our descent into utter Sissitude like those two little words "That's offensive." The American Sissy deploys those two pusillanimous, self-righteous, schoolmarm words the way Polynesians use *tabu* or Muslims pronounce other Muslims *kafir*. As trump card and conversation ender, "offensive" is the more vague, all-purpose, and sissitudinous version of morally front-loaded words like "racist," "sexist," "denialist," all the other ists, "homophobic" and "anti-Semitic." They're an easy, lazy, passive-aggressive way to assume the moral high ground, to put another person instantly on the defensive, sent to the shame corner, shunned by polite society.

Americans used to have what the Supreme Court defined as "fighting words." Now we just have this "offensive speech." In the old America, to offend someone was an action. There was intent. "Offend" was a transitive verb, with a specific subject at one end and a specific object at the other. American A offended American B. It was then up to American B to respond. He could choose to ignore it, he could offend back, or he could break a bottle over A's head.

Now the verb "offend" has been softened-and-squished into the passive, Sissy adjective "offensive." American B no longer says, "You have offended me," because then the burden of response is on B, and Sissies don't like to be personally responsible for anything. No, now American B sniffs, "That's offensive." A doesn't have to intend to offend B, or anyone else. B doesn't even have to be personally offended. Now it is just generically "offensive." The entire transaction has been lifted from the realm of personal interaction, which Sissies loathe, into some vastly more vague sphere of socially engineered politically correct passive aggression. The burden of action—to ignore, or offend back, or smash a bottle over A's head—has been lifted from B, and shifted to A. Now the onus is on A, who may or may not have intended to offend anyone by speaking a word that B finds offensive.

Now that A stands accused of offensive speech, the Napoleonic code applies. Once you accuse someone of being a racist or a homophobe or an utterer of offensive language, he's guilty of it until he can prove his innocence. And what is he guilty of? Incorrect speech. Bad thoughts. Improper attitudes. In that case, how can he prove his innocence? He can't. He can only accept or reject his guilt. If he rejects it, he's obviously guilty anyway. Only a racist would refuse to defend himself against charges of racism. Only a denialist would deny his denial. It's like the medieval test for witchcraft of dunking the accused under water. If she was a witch, she'd float. If she wasn't a witch, she'd drown. Either way, she was screwed.

In today's witch hunt, the person accused of some ism usually accepts his guilt. He must then make a public apology and submit to a public shaming. He might also, depending on how securely his accusers have seized the moral high ground, be expected to undergo a legally mandated program of brainwashing and reeducation, aka "sensitivity training." This will wash away the bad thoughts and attitudes, and the guilty ism-ist emerges like a newly baptized Christian from the waters of the Jordan, sinless and stainless. If the cure takes, A will never again utter any speech that B may find somehow offensive.

It's not just the PC liberals who use this conversation-stopping Sissy tactic. If a "liberal" doesn't want to hear what a "conservative" is saying, he calls it offensive. If a "conservative" doesn't want to hear what a "liberal" is saying, he calls it politically correct.

Both are euphemistic ways of saying, "I think you're wrong, and I don't want to hear it." It's the equivalent of sticking your fingers in your ears and going LAH LAH LAH LAH LAH until the other side gives up. This way neither has to think about what the other is saying. Neither is put in the embarrassing position of actually having to answer the other, to counter, to engage in actual debate. We don't have debate in this country anymore. We only have forums for broadcasting one-sided opinionating. Conservatives have FOXNews and talk radio. Liberals have NPR and the *New York Times*. Both sides are too Sissy to really listen to each other, to think about what the other says, to maybe rethink or at least have to articulate their own side. We not only don't debate, we don't even really argue anymore. We just shout over each other from our separate soapboxes. We hear only the side we like, and block out the other.

I encountered a classic example of this kind of not-listening and not-thinking recently. I was waiting for a friend in a bar one evening when an older man and a younger man sat themselves down in the stools next to me and ordered a couple beers. They seemed related somehow—maybe father and son, or more likely father-in-law and son-in-law.

"So," the younger man says, "I listened to some NPR like you suggested."

"Yeah? What did you think?" the older man gruffed. "Great, right? The only intelligent voices on the whole damn radio."

The younger man cleared his throat. "Well, I liked it all right. But it did all start to sound the same. Same voices, same opinions. I guess it just seemed a little one-sided."

"So?" the older man growled. "They're the right side."

"Well, I guess I just like to hear all sides of an argument and make up my own mind."

"What, you mean those asshole conservative talk-show people? I never listen to them. NPR is the only station on my dial."

"I'm not saying I agree with them. But don't you at least want to hear what they say?"

"NO!" the older man thundered. He smacked the bar, making their beer glasses jump. "I listen to NPR because they're right and I agree with them! I don't want to hear other opinions! I already know I disagree with them! Why should I listen to what they have to say?"

The younger man opened his mouth, blinked a couple of times, and gave up. He knew when to shut up and drink his beer.

That old man is what I call a *fundamentalist liberal*. He accepts the word of NPR as absolute truth and divine revelation, exactly the way fundamentalist Christians read the Bible.

For a while I dated a girl I called Anvil Head. Not to her face. I have my Sissy moments, just like anyone else. Once Anvil Head made up her mind about anything, no contravening facts could dent it. You could bang on that mind with the Ballpeen of Truth until you dropped from exhaustion, it wouldn't make any difference. Anvil Head had a *fundamentalist faith* in her correctness that rendered all discussion moot. It was one of those relationships that begin in misery and end in disaster.

Because we hear all the time about Christian and Muslim fundamentalism, we think of it as a religious trend. It is in fact an intellectual, social, and political one. Or, to be more precise, an *anti*-intellectual, antisocial, and political one. And profoundly antidemocratic and, in its full flowering, totalitarian.

Because of its great appeal to the American Sissy, fundamentalism has swept the land. And I don't mean just the Christian version. Americans of the liberal secularist persuasion enjoy telling themselves that the only fundos in this country are those awful evangelical Christians who want to turn the nation into a repressive theocracy. I happen to agree that those people are a real problem for our society. I think foreign Muslim fundamentalists are a smaller long-term threat to *my* Homeland Security than homegrown Christian fundamentalists are, and their ignorant, bellicose, and self-righteous political maneuverings need to be countered by a reinvigorated spirit of open-minded free-thinking if we don't want America to become a Christian Taliban nation.

But the Christians are hardly the only fundamentalists in our society. Rigid, mindlocked, sanctimonious fundamentalist groupthink has spread to all areas of our society, including those so-called liberal humanists who *used* to advocate open-minded freethinking.

If you have turned your political positions or social views into *matters of faith*, you're a fundamentalist. If you accept what your pundits or your preachers or any kind of gurus or authority figures tell you as unassailable absolute truth, you're a fundamentalist. If you cite the *New York Times* or Bill O'Reilly or "the scientific community" or "expert consensus" the way Christians cite the Bible, you're a fundamentalist. If you're a head-bobbing, knee-jerking groupthinker who's closed ranks with any political or social or religious or identity group and closed your mind and stopped thinking or questioning or doubting or listening, you're a fundamentalist. If you demonize and viciously attack any individual or group with opinions or beliefs different from or in opposition to your group's, you're a fundamentalist.

When you think about fundamentalism that way, it's obvious how widely and deeply it's taken hold in America. This country is lousy with Anvil Heads who have crossed the line from having deeply held political opinions or well-thought-out positions on social issues to become True Believers for whom politics or social issues are *belief systems, matters of unquestioned and unshakable faith.*

They're everywhere. PETA people are, obviously, furndamentalists. Their incredibly self-righteous zealotry about "kindness to animals" gives them all sorts of license to be unkind to people. They've forgotten that people are animals, too.

There are global warming fundos, people who don't just believe that global warming is happening, they believe *in* global warming, the same way certain evangelical Christians believe in Armageddon and the Rapture. It's an apocalyptic, millenarian religion for them. They cite "the scientific community" to defend their faith in exactly the way Christians cite the Bible to defend theirs. They shut out contrary scientific analysis the same way creationists shut out evolution. They know the truth, they've already had the truth handed down to them, they can quote you the truth chapter and verse. If you haven't heard the Word and accepted Al Gore into your heart, shame on you, you're a right-wing dildo the corporate capitalists are using to fuck Gaia up the ass.

There are fundamentalist Democrats and fundamentalist Republicans, people for whom party affiliation is a secular religion. They don't merely think the leaders and members of the opposing party are terminally wrongheaded, they truly believe they're evil. And they believe the flipside, that the leaders of their own party are, by definition, righteous and good, no matter what they do. You know the kind of people I'm talking about. You may be one of them. Republicans for whom Bill Clinton's blow-jobs were evil, but who have blithely shrugged off the death and destruction George W. Bush has sowed around the world. Democrats for whom the entire Bush administration is evil incarnate, but who passionately defended Clinton's unconscionable narcissism, his lying to their faces and his breezy destruction of the career and reputation of a young female employee for the sake of those blowjobs. Every guy has gotten a few blowjobs he had to lie about. But not as the president of the United States, not in the Oval Office, and not on national TV.

Many American Zionists are fundos. If you question or criticize any policy or activity of the Israeli government at all, they shriek loathsome charges of anti-Semitism or neo-Nazism. They're beyond touchy, beyond fanatical—they're fundamentalists. They even slandered Jimmy Carter, than whom no American president tried to do more to broker peace and stability for Israel, denouncing him as an anti-Semite for criticizing Israel's policies toward the Palestinians. Like only an anti-Semite or a Nazi could watch Israel cluster-bomb Lebanese women and children or build a new Berlin Wall around the West Bank and think, "Huh. That doesn't seem quite right somehow..."

Because of how and when and whom it first struck, AIDS quickly became the most politicized and most emotionally charged health issue of our time. Not the only, surely, but the most. It also became a secular religion. No doubt the way many so-called religious people in America originally responded to AIDS—as God's punishment for the wickedness of the queers, ho's, and drug addicts—helped push things in that direction. Whatever the reason, the church of AIDS developed an orthodoxy, a zealotry, a martyrology, and an unshakable faith in its own righteousness. As with global warming, True Believers accept everything the health industry decrees about AIDS exactly the way religious fundos believe every word in the Bible or the Koran is divine revelation. Anyone who questions the orthodoxy or proposes any alternative is demonized and vilified with the ugly label "AIDS denialist."

I'm not an AIDS denialist. I also don't deny that the weather has been getting pretty End of Days lately, or that 6.6 billion humans must be having an impact on the environment. I certainly don't deny Israel's right to exist. I sure do deny that it's right for any knee-jerk, groupthinking Sissy-fascists to label and libel me, or anyone else, just for raising a hand to ask a question. I sure do reserve the right to maintain an open mind, and to listen to all sides of any issue. I most heartily support the right of any individual, in all sectors of our public life, to speak, to doubt, and to question. When I was in high school the Jesuits taught us a Latin saying we called the Ooby Dooby proverb: *Ubi dubium ibi libertas.* Where there's doubt, there's liberty.

Listen, if you accept what *any* figures of authority say—whether that's scientists, media, PETA, professors, Larry Kramer, Al Gore, or the pope—with the same unthinking, unwavering faith that fundamentalist Christians and Muslims have for the Bible and the Koran, you are, at the very least, naive, and most likely a mental and emotional infant. Any adult with two brain cells to rub together knows that no human—not the scientists, not Bill O'Reilly, not the pope or whoever wrote the Bible and the Koran—is infallible. And that very few "truths" are absolute.

Why have fundamentalist attitudes swept the land of the American Sissy? For one thing, *they absolve you of the terrible responsibility to have an original, critical, or independent thought.* Ever. All your thinking has been done for you by your authority figures and handed down to you as the Word. All you have to do is bob your head and jerk your knee. You never have to think about that issue again. It's been prethought for you. The American Sissy loves being handed a free pass to the No Think Zone. Thinking is hard. Believing is easier. In a culture that does such a lousy job training people in math, science, reading comprehension, and general problem solving, it's no wonder that thinking is devalued while rigid belief and mindlocked faith are on the rise. The American Sissy is highly suspicious of people who don't take things as matters of blind faith, people who think too much, have doubts, ask too many questions. They are troublemakers, skeptics, cynics, denialists, conspiracy theorists, ass pains, brain aches.

Fundamentalism also appeals to Sissies because *it offers an easy and readily accessible high horse to climb on,* all saddled up and mad for a gallop. Americans love climbing up on their high horses and riding them around. Much of what passes for public discussion and debate in this culture is really just opposing sides competing in a race to the moral high ground. You know how when some-body rear-ends your car, then leaps out and starts doing an orangutan dance in the street, screaming at you as though it was your fault? It's a classic tactic meant to disarm you and sow doubt. You're supposed to go, "Hm, well, maybe this shouting lunatic has a point. Maybe I shouldn't have been sitting here in his way, waiting for the red light, when he came barreling down the street. Gosh sir, I'm sorry. Here's my insurance company."

Fundamentalists use a smug, self-righteous assumption of moral superiority in the same way. It's not because they're so secure in the knowledge of their own righteousness. It's because, like that guy who rear-ended you, they're so *insecure* in their righteousness. Their smugness, their slanders, are tactics for heading off any actual debate or discussion before it can happen. They don't want to have to debate, because to debate you have to think. They're not thinkers. Not-thinking is one of the perks of being True Believers.

Christopher Hitchens recently came to New York City to participate in a public debate about George W. Bush's wars. Half the audience was young antiwar protesters who came to drown him out shouting bumper sticker slogans at him until he gave up and walked off the stage. Like that old guy I overheard at the bar, they felt they already knew what he was going to say and that they wouldn't like it, so why listen? Regardless of my opinions about Hitchens, if I'd gone to hear him debate I sure as hell wouldn't have wanted to hear a bunch of American Taliban shouting bumper stickers instead.

Something similar happened at Columbia University around the same time. In fact, student groups shout down any speech they don't want to hear on colleges campuses all around the country all the time. Do we wonder why so many of our young people are such smug, close-minded idjits? *We've been training them to be that way in our so-called institutions of higher learning for thirty years.* Instead of math, science, reading comprehension, and general problem solving. We were too busy divvying up the academic spoils by identity group, so that only African Americans can study—excuse me, "celebrate"—African Americans in sistory, and only feminists can celebrate women in sistery, and only horses and pigs can write about agriculture. We were so busy teaching kids to celebrate their grievances about their identity as victims that they don't know shit, but they sure can cop a righteous tude. Good job, Professor Sister Right-on.

It would be one thing if fundamentalists held and shared their dogmatic beliefs among themselves, but they don't. Fundamentalism means proselytizing and politics. Fundamentalists aren't content just being fundamentalists themselves. They want to turn the whole world fundo-mental. If you made a documentary you could call it *Stoopitize Me.* Or, *Have You Been Slaved?*

The Christian and Muslim versions are reactions against modernism, Darwinism, secularism, liberalism, democracy, and science—all of which the Muslim fundos sum up as Westernism. Both versions are headlong retreats away from knowledge and science and human progress and individual freedom to a premodern mindlock where everything you know or do is dictated by the Bible or the Koran. Neither is content to climb into the Wayback Machine alone. They want to cram all the rest of us in there with them. All of society, and all the people in it, must conform to their dogmatic views. The Christians, being American Sissies, have mostly just putzed around with the existing political system and brainwashed their own children. The Muslims have gone balls out, dragging whole societies back in time, turning Iran, Saudi Arabia, Afghanistan into full-fledged totalitarian fundamentalist theocracies. It'd be fun to see someone like Mullah Omar get his hands on the leaders of the Christian right.

"You want to go back in time, motherfuckers? I got your sixth century right here."

You don't have to be antireligion to be antifundamentalism, because fundamentalism isn't religion. The world's great religions all preach pretty much the same basic code of conduct, and it's not a bad one to drill into the head of the human ape. Be kind and respectful to others. Don't fuck with them or their shit. Try to do good and not do bad. Who's not down with that? Christian and Muslim fundamentalism are not among the world's great religions. They are among the world's wacky, reactionary, totalitarian political movements. People who think they're antireligion like to cite all the evil that men have done throughout history in the name of organized religion. But maybe the problem isn't the religion, it's the organization. Men have done lots of evil in the name of organized politics and organized commerce and even organized sports. A good anarchist argument could be made that anytime more than two people get organized, their capacity to do evil is multiplied tenfold.

It does give me an idea for a movie, though.

It's about an enterprising reality TV producer in the near future who fences off an area of the Arizona desert and fills it with knives, clubs, spears, brass knuckles. Fundamentalist contestants locked into the area fight it out. Christians v. Muslims, Zionists v. Hindus, etc. It is soon the most popular program in the world.

Cue announcer:

Islam or Isn't Lam? Will Mohammad spill the Blood of Jesus? World. War. III. It's on. Tonight on

Armed * A * Geddon™
Two Faiths Enter. One Faith Leaves...
And lives to fight again next week.

I see John Carpenter directing. The sequel is a no-brainer: *Escape from Armed*A*Geddon.*

Okay, let's take another call.

Sissy: "Oh come on. PETA nuts and those college kids are annoying but they're not the Taliban. Jerry Falwell was a smug, smarmy porker but he was no Hitler."

Me: True enough. But fundamentalists of all sorts still actively campaign to limit or deny your rights—your right to free speech, to free thought, even to expensive fashion. Their impulses are fascist. It's a soft, Sissy fascism, but that's only because they lack the political and military muscle to go all the way.

Sissy fascists tell you that whatever they're trying to force you to think or do is *for your own good.* They're saving your soul, saving the life of your unborn child, saving you from AIDS, saving the planet.

Danke schön, mein Führer.

★ ★ ★

Fundamentalist knee-jerk is one driver of a wider problem: *The Sissy is a craven conformist.* There's not much the Sissy won't think, do, or say if all the other Holsteins are thinking, doing, or saying it. No matter how stoopit, ridiculous, immoral, or destructive the herd behavior is, the Sissy will join in. If a Sissy walks into a room full of people standing on their heads it's not long before he convinces himself he's upside down. If two Sissies take a long elevator ride together, they start to mutate and merge. They come out of the elevator looking exactly the same. Same haircut, same clothes, everything. That's why when you look in a restaurant everybody inside looks the same. Put that many Sissies in a room together and they all mutate and meld to blend in to be indistinguishable from one another. The last thing the American Sissy wants is to stand out among or be distinguishable from other Sissies.

In a classic series of psychology experiments conducted in the 1950s, subjects in groups were shown a set of lines and asked to pick out the one that was a different length from the others. The answer was obvious. But the actual test subjects were surrounded by a majority of ringers who were in on the experiment, and these ringers intentionally picked the wrong line. Even though the test subjects could clearly see this was the incorrect answer, most of them went along with the crowd and picked the wrong line anyway. They didn't want to go against the group, to be seen as different or difficult.

You might think yeah, well, that was the '50s. But numerous

tests over the decades since have yielded similar results. Quite often, people would simply rather be wrong than stand out from the crowd. They'd rather go along with the wrong, stoopit answer than speak up. This could be stated as a law: *For the Sissy, if it comes down to morality versus normality, normality wins.*

Even our outlaws and rebels are go-along-to-get-along conformists. They travel in packs—street gangs, biker gangs, skinheads—complete with color-coded uniforms. Are you gangstas or cheerleaders?

How did this happen? Americans were once infamous around the world as the precise opposite of conformist sissies. We were Yankees, pioneers, frontiersmen, cowboys and Indians; John Henry and Jack Johnson; Calamity Jane and Mae West. Even our losers and outlaws and misfits had character and individuality. Americans' image of themselves, the American idea and ethos and mythos, the American Dream—the whole point of America, really—was focused on the individual and the family. Not the team, the tribe, the herd, the pack. It was all about the individual citizen, the individual soul, individual rights, abilities, skills, goals.

Yes, for vast numbers the American Dream was just that—a dream, and a damn cruel one. For a long time, women, blacks, the Irish, and others need not apply. And the Puritans were in there from early on, screwing things up with their look-alike, knee-jerk groupthink. The original American Sissies and proto-Taliban. We have a lot to blame them for.

Still, it was a goal, an ideal, and it drove the building of the nation and the empire of America. For better or worse, we were, all of us, one way or another, always looking to the future and lighting out for the hinterlands, whether those were geographical, intellectual, entrepreneurial, spiritual, or emotional. We pioneered a nation and a culture from scratch. It was loud, brash, sometimes brutal, and often vulgar, but it was also adventurous, inventive, and rich with potential for individual achievement and fulfillment. People poured in from around the world to be a part of it. Success and fulfillment were in no way guaranteed, but you could try, and if you had the skill and the luck you might make it. Just the possibility, the dream, was a lot more than you were offered in a lot of other places.

There's not much of that individual initiative and adventurousness left in Sissy Nation. Its loss first became widely evident after World War II. Even as the American empire was reaching the height of its wealth and power, the last of the brash, brawling empire builders were dying off. They left the empire, fully formed and functional, to their useless descendants, who grew fat, decadent, and Sissified in it. Unlimited prosperity and great power have a way of doing that. Ask the Chinese, the Romans, the British, the Eloi. We turned inward and distracted ourselves with increasingly frivolous pleasures and pursuits, devolving toward our present state of Sissiness. Unable to think or act for ourselves, unable even to imagine living a rich and fulfilled life, we began to eat to obesity and surround our soft, squishy inner-Sissy cores with cocoons of expensive toys and ridiculous luxuries.

Why did this start in the postwar years? For one thing, Americans who had lived through the deprivations of the Depression and the horrors of World War II were really, really ready to settle down and have a nice, quiet life, with a nice house on a nice, quiet street, and a secure job to pay for it. It seemed a small price to pay to live in anonymous suburbs in identical houses and wear identical outfits to interchangeable jobs. Who could blame them?

In his 1956 best seller *The Organization Man*, William H. Whyte Jr. described another powerful engine driving us all into the herd. Early American capitalism was a game for real men and women, for entrepreneurs and risk takers, where anybody with vision and balls and a bit of dumb luck could, theoretically, thrive and prosper. Early capitalism made each citizen an individual capitalist with a shot at the brass ring. This ideal of capitalism, based on individual skills, entrepreneurship, and the Protestant work ethic, began fading away by the 1880s, as corporations grew and took over larger and larger segments of the economy. The American economy shifted from farming to industry, from rural to urban. This meant that fewer and fewer of us were self-reliant pioneers and husbandmen and inventors and entrepreneurs, able to grow and make things for ourselves. We were becoming worker bees and consumers, relays in the great corporate chain of being, exchanging our time on the factory floor or in the office cubicle or behind the sales counter for goods and services provided by, of course, the corporations. It's no coincidence that the first brand marketing—Ivory soap led the way in America—began in the 1880s.

By the 1950s when Whyte was writing, the transformation was complete. American capitalism *was* corporate consumerist capitalism, and we had all become interchangeable parts in giant corporate combines, as worker bees or consumers or both. Obviously, this affected more than just business and work: it transformed our whole society, our lives, and our ideal of ourselves as Americans. Whyte summed up the new prevailing ethic: "Man exists as a unit of society. Of himself, he is isolated, meaningless; only as he collaborates with others does he become worthwhile, for by sublimating himself in the group, he helps produce a whole that is greater than the sum of its parts."

Funny how Soviet that sounds, given that another great driver of conformism in the '50s was our fear of communism and our Cold War paranoia that we might be infiltrated, invaded, or downright annihilated by the Rooskies. It was especially the fear of infiltration, of *infection* by foreign bodies and foreign ideas, that fueled the witch hunts and show trials of McCarthyism. Fear of being suspected as one of those viruses of communism certainly was an influence on the look-alike me-tooism of the era.

It's no coincidence that the movie *Invasion of the Body Snatchers* appeared the same year as Whyte's book. In the movie, alien seed pods from outer space land in a small California town and begin replacing the inhabitants with identical duplicates. The clones look exactly like the individuals they replace, but they don't think or act like individuals. They're all interconnected through a hive brain that determines all of their behavior. They have no individual spark, no identity separate from the hive. In fact, as the invasion proceeds, the remaining humans in town give themselves away by betraying independent thought.

Because the movie and the novel on which it was based were released in the Cold War 1950s, the insidious replacement of human individuals with hive-brain clones has often been interpreted as a political metaphor. Some see it as a warning about the spread of communist collectivist ideology; others see the opposite, a metaphor for the spread of a Red Scare McCarthyite herd mentality.

For the record, the makers of the film always denied that they intended any political message. And in fact it's easier and better to see the film as a metaphor for a larger and ultimately more dreadful problem than mere left-wing or right-wing politics. It's about a general loss of individuality and independence—the ease with which the American Sissy gives up free will and unique personality in exchange for the comforts of being absorbed into the group, the tribe, the Sissy herd.

When we look back from half a century's distance, one of the most interesting results of Whyte's research was that the young company men he met (they were almost uniformly men in those days, with "company wives") were in no way helpless managerial slaves who'd been swallowed up by the growing corporate Moloch (see the silent movie *Metropolis*). They were contented cogs in the corporate wheel, happy to identify themselves as company men, and just as happy to identify *with* the company. They truly believed that by contributing, each in his own anonymous, inter-changeable way, to the overall good of the corporate hive, they were improving their own lives and everyone else's. GE and Mon-santo really were going to make the world a better place, and they were proud to be a part of it. The hive rewarded their loyalty with the promise of a secure job and a pension at the end of it.

Their children and grandchildren, the yuppies from the go-go 1980s to the present, could only dream of such a steady, secure existence. The rules changed in the 1980s, and corporations became the opposite of the safe, secure, buzzing hives they'd been. Now the ever shifting corporate environment created the insecurity and anxiety that made yuppies so defensively egoistic, cynical, and fatalistic, and such stressed-out fearful Sissies.

To people in the 1960s and '70s, the '50s looked like a uni-formly conformist era. But it was also the decade of teenage rebellion, rock 'n' roll, progressive jazz, Abstract Expressionism, and the Beats, all of which laid the groundwork for the more overtly rebellious '60s. Looking back from the 2000s, we can see that the 1950s got a bit of a bad rap. We may not be Organi-zation Men and Women anymore, but we are all Gap Kids. We conform now through consumption. We may be wearing hoodies and baggy jeans instead of gray flannel suits, but we're just as anonymous and interchangeable as ever. And we're completely content to be so.

You want an example? Look at your car. Just look at it. Now look at your neighbor's. Can you tell them apart? In the '50s, the '60s, into the '70s, your car was an individual statement. Your car had style, character, panache. It had curves and edges, came in a myriad colors, and could be personalized in a million ways. The annual unveiling of new models was anticipated with genuine excitement. When I was a kid, part of the fun of a long highway drive was looking at all the different kinds of cars and trucks on the road. On long drives, parents used to coax bored kids into playing a game where you had to spot five or ten of the same car. It could take hundreds of miles to win.

Now the game would be over before they got down the block. Everybody drives the same car, the Generica. It looks soft and formless, with no defined features or character, and—god forbid—no sharp edges on which a Stoopit might hurt himself. It looks less like a fully formed car than a car fetus. Like the designer didn't have time to carve the model out of his bar of Ivory soap and just handed in the bar of soap. There are no colors, only gray, black, or white. Colors are reserved for those naughty "sport" models. Even the most pimped-out rides look store-bought. You go on long highway drives now, and every Generica around you looks just like the Generica you're in. They could have bar codes on them.

You can't work on them yourself anymore, either. This happened at the same time as the genericizing. Before the Generica, when you opened the hood of your car you saw a recognizable internal combustion engine. It was iron and steel and wiring. It was mechanical. With a little bit of training—I got mine from my dad, like most kids in my day—you knew which parts did what, so when it failed to function in a certain way, you had an idea of which parts to check. With a minimum of cheap Sears tools you could tighten, loosen, replace, or just whang on it in frustration, and get the thing running again. I had a car I kept on the road for a few years with a pair of pliers, a screwdriver, and duct tape. By the end the whole thing was duct-taped together. It was butt ugly but it ran.

All of that—not just the knowledge but the self-reliance, too—has been taken away from you with the Generica. Now you lift the hood of your car and it's like lifting the casing off your computer. The Generica's engine looks like a vacuum cleaner from the starship *Enterprise*. You need a Ph.D. from DeVry and a million dollars in diagnostic equipment to work on it. So most of us don't even try. If something goes wrong, we ask The Man to fix it for us. Don't you find that demoralizing? And emasculating? And Sissifying? I don't mean that in the good old days every American could shoe his own horse or fix his own car, but the difference now is that you couldn't even if you wanted to, because the capacity has now been lifted completely beyond you. The horse doesn't wear horseshoes anymore. It's equipped with Fully Integrated Quadrupedal Equine Vehicle-to-Ground Interfaces. You can't change them. And *you don't want to anyway*. You've got online games to play.

We are, in fact, totally surrounded by and utterly dependent on machines, appliances, and services that we have absofuckinglutely no idea how they work. Telephones, televisions, computers, iPods, cars, the plumbing, the heat, the A/C, the lights, the oven, the fridge, the toaster, all of it. The American Sissy in his crib is as helpless and clueless as an infant in *his* crib. This infantilization has been in process for a long time, a slow and gradual encroachment of once undreamed-of goods and services that are now absolute necessities, making us increasingly helpless and dependent even as they improve our lives. And all of them have been, undeniably, improvements to our standard of living. Okay, most of them. The leaf blower and the car alarm are just noisy ways to annoy your neighbors, as are cell phones, the way most people use them most of the time, and of course their ringtones. Also, most anything advertised on TV as the "quick and easy" answer to opening a can of dog food, chopping a head of lettuce, or growing flowers or tomatoes is just slapping us in the face with our terminally lazy, decadent Sissiness.

But the rest of them are definitely improvements. I love computers. If I had to go back to banging away on my old Edsel-size Underwood, or trudging to the public library with every research question, I think I'd give up writing. I carry a cell. I got it for work, but I use it to have the same dumbass personal conversations in public that all other dumbass cell phone users use theirs for. I could live without it. I could live without Netflix, too, and the dishwasher in my apartment, and the electric coffee grinder. But I like them.

The thing is, I don't have a clue how they work. And when they don't work, I'm helpless. And since we're all dependent on them, they *should* work, all the time. You should be able to bring home a new computer and plug it in and have it work instantly, like a toaster. You don't have to spend hours on the phone with some toaster geek in Mumbai to get the toaster to toast bread. It just does. You shouldn't have to do it with your computer, either. It's not just the Revenge of the Nerds, it's the Holocaust of the Geeks.

But computers are just the leading edge. We don't know how *any* of it works, and we are increasingly dependent on and subservient to the geeks and experts just to get through our daily lives. How many American Sissies does it take to screw in a lightbulb? Zero. We don't do it ourselves, we call the 24-hour emergency line at Bulb World and they send over a Lighting Systems Management guy to do it for us. He has a degree in it from DeVry.

We have already been divided into two groups, the ones who own all the shit and the ones trained to make all the shit work. In the near future I believe we will have devolved into two separate species. There will be the Humans, boneless blobs of protoplasm puddling at the bottom of climate-controlled cradles like giant oysters with google eyes, all bodily functions biometrically maintained as they work and fight and fuck and live entirely in virtual space. All the maintenance will be done by genetically bottle-bred Humules, each trained in one specific task.

Now go look in your closet. Admit it—you bought these clothes because they're just like the clothes all your friends and neighbors wear. You all bought them at the same mall, or store, or from the same catalogue. Your clothes aren't merely in the same style as your neighbors', they proudly display the same logos. You are not simply conformist Sissies, you are *brand loyal* Sissies.

Has any virtue, at any time in the existence of humanity, been so debased as this descent from loyalty to *brand* loyalty?

It's true that there's absolutely nothing new about conforming to fashion. Throughout human history, fashion has been symbolic of your tribe, your caste, your class, your status. Fashion has always been a supremely conformist concern. It was Sissy millennia before the first Fashion Week gaystravaganza. The uses of fashion as a clear marker of status have been so well recognized that many societies have passed laws, called sumptuary laws, regulating who could wear what. In Elizabethan England, the merchant class got so wealthy they could easily afford to dress like lords and ladies. Elizabeth made it illegal. Proper British Victorians restricted themselves to an extremely narrow fashion code; it's not just because we see them in old photos that they're always in black and white.

We don't have any laws forcing us to dress according to our stations—although if you ride a New York subway wearing bling some other kid thinks is above your station, he may attack you for it. We don't need the laws because we do it ourselves. You yuppie males all wearing identical khaki slacks and brown loafers and pastel tennis shirts with the collars turned up. You yuppie females who grew up on *Sex and the City* in your identical short black skirts and identical dyed and straightened blonde hair and surgically identical little noses permanently turned up at the world. You wannabe gangstas—black, white, Asian, and Other— in your identical clown costumes, the baggy pants with the crotch between your knees so that you shuffle around like Stepin Fetchit kicked in the balls, and your sneakers that cost more than your parents pay in rent every month, and your XXXXXXXXL t-shirts that six of you could fit in shoulder to shoulder.

Hipsters, rockers, golfers, cyclists—we all use fashion the way street gangs and biker gangs use their colors: to make our tribal allegiance perfectly clear.

Yes, there are people who just, you know, wear clothes. But most of us wear uniforms. I don't mean the uniforms many of us wear to work—waitress and fireman outfits, lawyers' dark suits, bull-riders' Stetsons, or rap artists' shiny teeth. I mean the fashion uniforms we wear by social convention. We wear them to show people like us that we are people like them, or to show people we want to be like that we want to be just like them. We dress for success, or dress to look like we're successful. We dress to look bad or cool. Whether it's bling or Burberry, out of a J Crew catalogue or a secondhand store, we're making a statement with our clothes—not, generally, a statement about ourselves as individuals, but about the group to which we either belong or want to belong. It's an act of submission and compliance to sumptuary laws that are no less rigid or unclear for being unwritten. Go anywhere people of any certain group congregate, observe with the eyes of a space alien or an anthropologist, and you'll be amazed at how uniform the attire is.

Sissy: "So how do I spot a Sissy?"

Me: Sissy has become so pervasive in our culture that there's no one Sissy "look"—although some looks are more obviously Sissy than others. Like that preppy-yuppie tennis shirt with the upturned collar, especially when accesorized by a sweater thrown over the shoulders European-style like a little cape. That's not only Sissy, it's just plain *sissy*.

I don't know about where you live, but here in New York City another stand-out Sissy look is the twenty-something Blogger Boy. Recently, while waiting for a meeting on Bleecker Street in lower Manhattan, I watched ten identical Blogger Boys walk past me in ten minutes. Blogger Boy is a thin, pale young white dude wearing flip-flops, cargo shorts, and a vintage t-shirt, usually with some "ironic" logo on it. His hair is short and touseled. He's got his laptop in the man-purse slung over his bony shoulder, because he's on his way to Starbucks, and he's always on his cell.

Then again, I have to confess I also saw five guys go by who looked an awful lot like...me. The magazine *New York*, which obsesses about fashion trends to a degree way beyond the unseemly, has identified my Sissy phenotype as "grups": adults who refuse to dress like grown-ups. Grups are in their thirties, forties, fifties and still dress like they're in their twenties. They're rarely seen not wearing blue jeans, sneakers, and a vintage clothing store shirt or t-shirt. They wear their hair, if they still have their hair, a little long, a reminder of the days when they rocked out, *maaaan*.

Guilty, okay? Let's move on.

Sissy: "It's not our fault! The giant corporations did this to us! We don't design the identicars, they do. We don't mass-market the look-alike clothes, they do. It's not our fault we're indistin-guishable. We tried to protest, but they even commodified our dissent!"

Me: That is neo-Marxist Sissy crap *and* whiny infantilism. The giant corporations aren't run by evil brains from outer space. *We* are the giant corporations. A lot of us participate directly as worker bees in the hive. A small elite of us get to participate in the actual running of the hive. And all the rest of us participate as consumers, avidly licking up the honey.

Which brings us back to brand loyalty. Brand loyalty makes passive, feed-tube-down-the-gullet consumers feel like old-fashioned freedom-of-choice customers. (There's a reason no one ever says, "The *consumer* is always right.") It's been around at some level for a long time, too. You may have thought of yourself as a Hathaway Man, or a Ford Family versus a Chevrolet Family, like today's Mac snob versus the PC prole. But from the demor-alizing designer jeans fad of the '80s to the lethal sneaker wars of the '90s to the sad vulgarity of the Cristal and Hummer '00s, we've accelerated downhill from being customers to consumers to label whores. We don't just identify with brands, we identify ourselves *by* our brands. We wear our corporate branding logos across our chests, our hats, our butts. One of the jokes of the film *Idiocracy* is that by the twenty-sixth century, we'll wear clothes made up entirely of large corporate logos. The joke, of course, is that this won't happen until five hundred years from now.

And it's not just the middle class who have the disposable income and frivolous time for this. Rich folks and poor folks are label whores now, too. Different labels, different price points, all whores.

"I'm an Anderson and Sheppard Man."

"We're a Popeyes Family."

Whatever.

The standard Sissy excuse is, again, that the evil giant corporations made you label whores. Pimp Daddy Inc. snatched you from the cradle, an innocent little heifer, force-fed you with aggressive marketing and saturation advertising until you were a filthy label ho, branded you, and turned you out on the street.

No.

They.

Didn't.

If advertising and marketing worked that effortlessly, they wouldn't have to spend so many zillions on it every day. Do you know anyone in advertising or marketing? Do their jobs look easy to you? Is that why they're so stressed and medicated?

It's infantile Sissy victimology to blame the corporations. It's like saying it's Mr. Whipple's fault that you need to make number two. Like blaming the Colonel because you let little Brianna eat that whole trashcan-size bucket of extra crispy all by herself.

We *like* being label whores. We *like* being branded. Good Holsteins. We like being able to buy an identity along with our sneakers, our jeans, our bespoke suit. The same way we like being handed what to think and what to believe and what opinions to have. (What, you think you're label whores only about your clothes?) We like being identifiable as a member of a tribe, even if it's something as superficial as the Footlocker Tribe or the We All Just Stepped Out of A J Press Catalogue Indians. We like to fit in, blend in, conform. All the big, bad pimp daddy corporations did was make it *quick and easy* for you. Advertising and marketing exploit and hope to channel your me-too herd mentality, but they did not create it and they don't force it on you.

Here's one way to tell you can't blame anyone but yourselves. When the tattoo and piercing fad began in the 1980s, it was as close to an underground, countercultural activity as you could have in America in the 1980s. The people involved described themselves as "modern primitives" and spoke of a "new tribalism." The ones I knew or read about weren't always very clear what they meant by all that, but they clearly were trying to mark themselves as a tribe *apart*, standing outside and in some way, if only superficially, rejecting the mainstream of Sissy conformist consumerism. A generally high level of thought and choice went into the designs. When I met the late Michael Wilson, who performed at Coney Island as the Illustrated Man, in 1990, he was close to reaching his goal of covering every inch of his skin, from the top of his shaved head to the soles of his feet, in tattoos. Even in lower Manhattan he caused a stir on the streets with his tattoo-covered face. He wore hundreds of designs yet could tell you the personal significance of each one.

Well, we all know what became of tattoos—and no giant corporation caused it. Sissy conformism did. When the Sissies saw that tattoos were hip and cool they all had to have one, too. By 2000 it was impossible to spot an American under thirty who did *not* have a tattoo. It passed from being a symbol of nonconformity to a badge of craven conformity. And, being conformist Sissies, they not only all had tattoos, they all had *the same tattoos*. Generica tattoos, bought off the rack the same way their sneakers and t-shirts and all their other brandings were. There was the band encircling the upper arm, in either a "tribal," Celtic, or barbed-wire theme. For females, there was the one that looked like a permanent ankle bracelet, and the hideous lower-back one that looked like a permanent thong line. If an American Sissy under thirty had any tattoos, there was a very good chance he had one or more of these three designs. They couldn't tell you what those tattoos *meant* to them. Only where they bought them.

It may be just as well that Wilson died in 1996. The Coney Island he knew was disappearing, too. Soon to be plowed under to make way for a generic Sandals-style seaside resort.

The Gapification of the tattoo illustrates a distinction the consumerist hipster Sissy universally fails to understand: the vast difference between being merely hip and being truly cool. A friend of mine likes to say, "Hip is to fashion as cool is to style." To him, hipness and fashion are superficial, ephemeral, and easily merchandized; cool is innate, and style is timeless. You can buy what's hip, but you can't buy cool. Hipsters being as craven in their superficially nonconformist conformity as any of the "unhip" people they sniff at, they must maintain constant surveillance of a galaxy of temporary and ever changing rules and regulations regarding what is currently hip and what is so five minutes ago. Some of the coolest people you meet are hopelessly out of fashion, have no idea what's considered hip at the moment, and couldn't care less.

Hipness is public; like any other type of branding, it does you no good to look hip if nobody's around to appreciate it. Hipness is Holstein herd mentality in loner wolf's clothing. There are legions of Sissy hipsters, wearing identical fashions, listening to the same music, reading the same blogs, crowding together in the hippest neighborhoods in their towns. But there are no coolsters, just cool individuals. Cool needs no outward validation. That's why truly cool individuals are so rare.

And always *individuals*. A lot of what we recognize as cool about cool people is that they retain some of those old qualities of individualism and independence. Cool people go their own way, make their own agenda, have their own dreams and visions, don't follow the herd. They're not necessarily rebels or eccentrics, just individuals. They're what hipsters could be, but will never become by imitation and impersonation. If you're trying to look and act cool, you aren't. It's an existential joint, yo.

I'll give you this much: Being an individual is never easy. It goes against our programming. Not our corporate programming. Our genetic programming.

Our ideal of ourselves is that we humans are different from all other species of animals in that each of us is a distinct individual, a unique personality, endowed with free will. We don't respond to the world out of instinct alone. We are capable of rational analysis. We don't always go with the herd and run with the pack but are able to stand apart and stand up for what we believe, guided by a personal code of philosophy, morality, and ethics.

Well, yeah, maybe, sometimes. But we are undeniably animals, a species of ape marginally more intelligent than our cousins the chimps and the bonobos (shut up, Christian Stoopits), and just like all the other animals we very often act out of instinct. And one of our strongest instincts, in fact one of the keys to our survival as a species for a long time, is the urge, the need, to be part of a group. Being a relatively small and weak species, we learned to cooperate and organize ourselves to get by. Being territorial and competitive for resources, we learned to think and act in terms of the "in-group" and "out-groups," and how to fear and hate all out-groups as enemies.

Success and survival hardwired the lesson into our genes. To be an independent individual, to stand alone and apart, is to be vulnerable, exposed, unprotected. Loneliness doesn't just make us sad; it scares the hell out of us. The worst punishment they can give you in prison is solitary confinement. Probably the only human who doesn't need to feel part of some group in some way is the sociopath.

But there's a crucial difference between feeling part of some group and being completely absorbed by the group. We're apes, not ants or fish. We're not supposed to swarm mindlessly but to cooperate freely as individuals. It's the difference between cooperation and co-optation, between getting organized for some purpose and just collecting in a herd, a mob, a swarm of Sissies.

At the end of *Body Snatchers*, the last human in town escapes and tries to warn the rest of humanity. We see him stopping traffic on a busy highway, crying, "Look, you fools. You're in danger. Can't you see? They're after you. They're after all of us. Our wives, our children, everyone. They're here already. *You're next!*"

Yes, indeed. We have met the look-alike Sissies, and they are us. Looking alike, dressing alike, thinking alike, acting alike. Bobbing our heads and bending our knees in unison. Believing what we're told to believe, and shunning anyone who believes otherwise.

Living a fulfilled life, thinking and acting for yourself, standing out from the crowd, embracing the new and the different rather than fearing it…it all takes work. It's a fact of human nature that even in this great democracy of ours, in which all people are free to form their own opinions and speak their own minds and pursue their own personal goals, many of us lack the will and opt for the ease and safety of herd behavior. As the alien clones explain to the last resisting humans in *Body Snatchers*, life is so much easier when you stop struggling and give in:

"There is no pain. Suddenly, while you're asleep, they'll absorb your minds, your memories, and you're reborn into an untroubled world… Tomorrow you'll be one of us… There's no need for love… Love. Desire. Ambition. Faith. Without them, life is so simple, believe me."

The film originally ended with that last man from the town hysterically shouting his warning to no avail. People just think he's a nut.

But the studio forced the director to tag on a false ending, in which the man convinces the authorities he's not crazy. They send in the troops and quash the alien invasion before it can spread.

Whew. Hooray for Hollywood.

In the real world, of course, the authorities are Sissies, too. If we look to the authorities to save us from Sissiness, we're all goners.

Yet who, really, is looking to be saved? How many brave individuals are gamely swimming against the tide of Sissy sameness?

I could name a few, but I won't. You'd just try to dress like them.

Everyone knows the Average American Male is completely useless. Curled up here inside the bubble of Sissitude and Stoopitness—inside Fundadome—he plays with his guns, some real, some imagined. He plays with his online friendsters. He plays air guitar and fantasy football. He plays with himself.

In terms of emotional maturity, the Average American Male never makes it out of high school. That crotchety old geezer tootling down the sidewalk in his go-cart chair with his Life Alert and laminated AARP card hanging from his neck is a boy inside his head.

American society used to be organized to force the American male at least to pretend to be a mature, responsible adult. He had to get a job, he had to get married, he had to be the breadwinner and bring home the bacon for the wife and kids. Specific days or hours were set aside for his playtime—almost always in the company of other males. He got to go on his fishing or hunting trips, watch football on Sunday, spend an hour at the bar sometimes after work. He looked forward to these free times the way he'd looked forward to the end of the school day and summer vacation. His woman knew that if he wasn't allowed this playtime he might go postal, or run away from home, or at the very least become mopey and resentful and even more useless to her.

Whatever else the institution of marriage ever was, it was *a system for forcing males to act like responsible adults.*

With the rise of the independent, wage-earning female, the simultaneous destruction of the family unit at the poverty end of the scale, the putting off of having kids or the decision to have none, the spread of alternative relationships, and the general de-emphasizing of the male's lifetime commitment to marriage and to being the sole financial support of a family, he has found himself under less and less pressure to pretend to be a mature, responsible adult. He has more playtime. He can, with an ease unknown in his grandfather's day, indulge his inner adolescent in perpetuity. He can surround himself with games and toys, fantasy sports and fantasy adventures and fantasy friendsters. Freed from having to pretend he's a responsible adult, he can pretend he's whatever his boyish heart desires. A gangsta, a pimp, a zombie-hunting space commando. It doesn't much matter if we play these roles at home, on the screen, or in the street. We're all Gameboy.

It's no wonder, then, that the Average American Male has become so confused about his masculinity and the role of masculinity in the Sissy world. He feels thoroughly pussy-whipped, not just by his own woman but by women generally. He is treated like a lazy idiot, useful only for heavy lifting and procreation. No wonder he has retreated into a state of perpetual adolescence. No wonder so many young black males try to live like hypermasculine cartoons (hypermasculinity is Sissiness with a severe complex), and so many young white males try to dress, act, and think like girls. Their mamas, girlfriends, and wives wear the pants in this society. There's a good reason "yo mama" jokes are ubiquitous but you never hear "yo papa" jokes. Papa just *is* a joke.

Yes, we all know about the glass ceiling in the boardroom, and that women's average salaries are lower than men's. Guys set it up that way on purpose, a long time ago. They built in disincentives to women joining them at the workplace. It was one place men could go and pretend to be boss. That's why they didn't want women in their bars and clubs, either. Men needed zones where they could pretend to be in charge, pretend to be organized, pretend to be independent, and generally look busy pretending to be busy.

"I'm in charge of this office."

"I'm the boss of this boilermaker. Gimme another, I'll boss that one around too."

Bartenders observed a cardinal rule: If a woman calls, you never, *ever* say, "Yeah, he's right here. Hold on." Girltenders knew the rule, too.

Girltenders were allowed because, same as secretaries, they pretended the men were boss.

Men needed these places because everywhere else in their lives the women were in charge and made no pretense about the men being the boss. Opening up the workplace to women—and to everyone else—was the right and proper thing to do, but it did eliminate it as a place where men could hide. No wonder they all headed out to the woods to bang their drums. Where the hell else were they going to go? Even country music went soft and girly as the "new Nashville" wooed the suburban moms. Good-bye hard-drinkin' truck-drivin' Southern Man, hello sensitive, Suburban-drivin' Soccer Dad. Meanwhile, women were let into the former male preserves of NASCAR, drag racing, the boxing ring, and the military, sealing the deal.

What's left? I'll tell you what's left. Those fake-fancy "gentlemen's" topless clubs with doofusy names like Scores and 10s and Foxes. The Average American Male drops fortunes in these joints. And for what? To watch putatively pretty fantasy women take off their shirts to show their plastic fantasy breasts. Woo hoo.

And for lap dances. Is there anything more demeaning than the lap dance? Not for the woman, for the *man*. The lap dance isn't about sex. It's interpretive modern dance illustrating the woman's total dominance of the male. The encounter is entirely in her control. A complete tease. He can get aroused, but he can't get no satisfaction. He can't kiss her, he can't even touch her, and it's for sure that if she gets him off it's going to be inside his shorts. The ultimate dry hump. How humiliating. And he pays top dollar for it. It'd be cheaper to marry her. Then she might actually have sex with him once a week.

Scores? It should be called You Won't Even Make First Base. Or Jagoff's.

These clubs have been designed specifically for the American Sissy. They are to real strip clubs what Internet porn is to peep booths, what the Generica is to real cars. They're clean, safe, generic, chained. They're Starbucks for Sissy sex. They're perfect examples of how *here inside Fundadome, virtually all reality has been turned into virtual reality.*

American Sissies are terrified of actual sexual contact, of the physical and emotional exposure. They feel much safer and more comfortable with Internet porn and places like Jagoff's than with actual intimacy.

The Sexual Revolution lasted only about a decade, from the general availability of the pill by the early '70s to the AIDS panic of the early '80s. American Sissies were never all that into orgies and swinging anyway, and never did get the point of the zipless fuck. Wasn't that what had given them blue balls all through adolescence? When it comes to sex, the American Sissy is anything but a revolutionary. Sissies were just trying to act like they enjoyed it because everyone told them they should. Good Holsteins. When the media started screaming at them that SEX = DEATH, the revolution shriveled up overnight. By the time it became apparent that the looming heterosexual AIDS epidemic had been just another one of those manufactured panics the social engineers whip up to stampede wandering Holsteins back into the barn, it was too late. Sex had shifted to the phone lines and the Internet, giving the zipless fuck a whole new meaning, and the American Sissy was much more comfortable having virtual sex anyway.

The truth is that even without AIDS, the Sexual Counter-revolution would have happened. As usual, Americans stoopitized the Sexual Revolution. Gay and straight, male and female, they made sex, one of the very most fun things humans can do, boring. Talk about a missed opportunity. Freed up to have all the sex they liked, American Sissies soon discovered they really didn't like sex all that much, at least not the sex they were having on their one-night stands and in Plato's Retreat and gay bathhouses. It was plastic sex, polyester sex, disco sex, anonymous sex, affectionless sex, meaningless sex. A dull, dispirited end-of-empire orgy. The sex they were having might as well have been Internet porn all along, for all the real human contact involved.

So the obedient American Sissy stopped having free sex, and started having Safe Sex. "Safe Sex" was an infantile euphemism for what used to be called wearing a rubber, but it was much more than that. Safe Sex was the kind of sex Sissies had been wanting to have all along. Sex without direct human contact. Sex without *exposure to danger.*

Our public health institutions don't harangue us about Safe Sex with the ferocity they used to, because it's become largely irrelevant. The Sissy has moved on from Safe Sex to virtual sex, fantasy sex, laptop and lap-dance sex. Sex couldn't get much safer.

There's nothing wrong with phone sex or Internet porn *per se.* If you feel like having sex and you've got no one to do it with, by all means do it yourself. The do-it-yourself spirit drove a lot of creativity and innovation in America's heyday. It's not bad that lonely, horny guys don't have to drag themselves to the sex shop or peep booths for DIY sex anymore. Those places were always designed to make men feel dirty and guilty, and they smelled like Mr. Clean had been in there jagoffing all over the walls and floor just before you got there. It's also a good thing that lonely, horny women have equal access to DIY sex and porn in the privacy of their own homes.

It's true that phone sex and Internet porn providers, like those gentlemen's clubs, way overcharge the Sissies to not-have sex, but that's just capitalism. It's also true that most of the folks who appear in porn are people you wouldn't want to watch stripping furniture, much less stripping off their clothes, but that's been a problem for pornographers since the daguerreotype.

The point is that phone sex and Internet porn aren't real sex, and they're no substitute for sex, no matter how many devices you hook yourself up to to make it seem like you're not just jag-offing. If you've done both you know the difference. Phone sex and Internet porn are to real sex as reality TV is to reality. If you're meeting people over phone lines or in chat rooms, you're not really meeting people. If you're talking or typing with them about having sex, you're not having sex. It used to be solely children and people with multiple personality disorder had imaginary friends. Now all the Sissies are having imaginary sex with theirs.

Sex without some degree of intimacy, of affection, of risk and exposure—of *actual human contact*—is just porn. Sissies don't have sex, they have porn. They're afraid to *have* sex, they only like to *watch* it. It's a performance. A fantasy. Role-playing. It doesn't much matter whether they're watching someone else having it, or themselves. Besides being safe, it feeds the narcissism that's a natural by-product of our infantilization. O baby o baby who's that pretty baby? It's *me*! Besides, if they went to college they've been taught to treat all sex, sexuality, and gender as fluid, a performance, a social construct foisted on them by The Man.

Let me put it this way. Have you had or been to a big wedding in the past decade? Weddings are no longer orchestrated to make the event itself enjoyable and memorable. They're organized around the crew making the wedding tape. Attending a wedding is like being on the set of an independent film. It's all about the lights, camera, and sound. Wedding guests are extras.

The bride and groom aren't there to get married, they're starring in the wedding video. They're role-playing the bride and groom for the camera. The wedding is just the necessary pretext. What they really want to do is come home from their virtual honeymoon—in some safe, generic, chained, virtual-vacation game preserve like Sandals or Club Med, the Scores and 10s of vacationlands, which will be like never leaving Fundadome at all—and watch themselves starring in the wedding video. Over and over again. Reliving the moment they never really lived in the first place. They're not living their lives, they're starring in their own movie adaptation of their lives.

See, here inside Fundadome, we fantasize obsessively about celebrity. We dream about what it would be like to be celebrities. We role-play it constantly. Only a handful of us get to make asses of ourselves role-playing it on *American Idol*, but the rest of us get to watch—the faux-celebuporn hit topped the Nielsen ratings in 2004, '05, '06, and '07. Real celebrities complain disingenuously about the paparazzi—and the world *adored* Princess Di for becoming a martyr to them—but in our hearts we all wish we had cameras following our every move as well. That's why young American Sissies can't seem to go anywhere or do anything now without documenting every second on their cell-cams. They make their own masturbatory paparazzi porn.

In the same way, American Sissies don't have sex to have sex. *They have sex so they can watch themselves having sex.* That's why almost all the porn on the Internet is amateur porn. The way reality TV pretends to be realer than TV, amateur porn is somehow supposed to be realer than porn. Many porn sites even advertise that they feature only "real amateurs." If that's not reality, what is? Like reality TV, amateur porn is entirely and unapologetically voyeuristic. Old porn, like un-reality TV, clung to traditional theatrical distinctions of audience and actors. Amateur porn, like reality TV, is snooping on your neighbors. In both, you're spying on them at their most exposed and vulnerable, whether they're in the throes of passion or in handcuffs for car theft. Amateur porn is one zone where the Internet comes through on its early promise to be a truly democratic medium. Call it a Plato's Retreat Republic. Just as all those high-speed car chases on reality TV have without a doubt inspired Stoopits to get into more high-speed car chases, the ocean of amateur porn makes it clear that no Sissies have sex anymore unless the camera's running.

But of course amateur porn is Sissy porn. For one thing, since it's all role-play anyway, and the Internet is an infinite warehouse of images, it's all been fetishized. Every fetish you can dream of, and a lot you never would, is available. There are sites specifically for anal, oral, threesomes, foursomes, older people, younger people, skinny people, fat people, foot people, blondes, redheads, people in uniform, people in latex, cartoon people, sex with midgets—I'm sorry, little people—sex with donkeys, sex with midget donkeys—I mean little donkeys… And it's all been tagged and taxonomied to make access quick and easy for Sissies and Stoopits.

The real Sissy giveaway is that almost no one making amateur porn, male or female, has pubic hair. In fact most of them have no hair on their bodies at all, except on their heads. Internet porn is like an infinite-loop commercial for Nair and the Brazilian wax. Pubic hair is so rare that it's a fetish, too, with sites devoted exclusively to "hairy" people—i.e., people who look like all human adults did before, say, 1990.

In a culture so infantilized, it's no surprise that Sissies want to look smooth and hairless as babies' bottoms. It's like they're retreating from their adulthood, and from sex, and from gender, and from their own humanity. It's permanent prepubescence.

When everybody's so smooth and hairless, it's hard to tell the boys from the girls. Their generic unisex tattoos don't help. But then, the ones who went to college and actually paid attention when the professors were preaching their confusion about gender and sexuality are hard to tell apart even with their clothes on. I see tons of young couples now who look like they've melted into each other—he's half-a-girl and she's half-a-boy and they both look neutered. They're not sure if they're straight or L, G, B, T, or a BLT on toast. The result is they're nothing definable at all, bland, limp blobs of protoplasm as unsexy and unsexed as sea monkeys.

Since all Sissy sex is fetishized fantasy and role-play, it makes sense that S&M, once a truly underground, behind-the-counter culture for connoisseurs of perversity, has been genericized and sissified into an activity about as bold and racy as...wearing a tattoo. It's Safe-Word Sex. There are S&M clubs on college campuses. They meet between the French Club and the Chess Club. Grown-ups have S&M organizations and associations they attend between swap meets and their kids' soccer practice. There's no real pain or degradation involved anymore, no real dominance or submission; it's all performance. Bad, boring, amateur performance. That's not S&M, it's S&K—Sexual Karaoke.

Naturally, these are boom times for makers of sex dolls and sexbots. Sex dolls and sexbots have a very long history. In Greek mythology, Pygmalion sculpted his perfect woman, Galatea, as the ancient equivalent of a sexbot. The philosopher René Descartes was rumored to be highly enamored of a mechanical doll in the form of a five-year-old girl he named Francine and carried with him in his trunk everywhere he traveled. I'm not saying he was a pedophile. I'm just saying. Sexy-but-scary robots have been all over the movies from as early as the 1927 *Metropolis* to the *Terminator* franchise. *Star Trek* reminded us often that Data was "fully functional" sexually.

There's always something melancholic in stories of lonesome humans consorting with animated but lifeless friends. It's easy to see what the philosopher Walter Benjamin was getting at when he called the clockwork doll a "relic of inscrutable loss." The same could be said for virtual sex and virtual relationships in virtual reality.

Gee, you start talking about sex and the calls pour in. Go ahead, Sissy.

Sissy: "If no one's really into sex, what about all those stories in the media about grade-school kids having blowjob parties? What about all the teen pregnancies? What's up with the hyper-sexuality in all those hip-hop videos?"

Me: Okay. In the first place, don't believe everything you read in the media, stoopit. Mass media have been peddling stories about the depravity of our young people since the invention of mass media nearly two hundred years ago. Every year as far back as I can remember some magazine has run a cover story announcing a new "trend" in teenage or adolescent sex. If it's news to you that adolescents and teens have sex, where were you when you were an adolescent and a teen?

Now, it is true that American adolescent and teenage girls get pregnant at double the rate of their peers in any other industrialized nation. It's not because American kids are twice as into sex as kids in other countries. It's because we've stoopitized them with our Sissy refusal to give them sex education and birth control. Nothing in American culture is stoopiter than hysterical adults believing that if they don't mention sex around their kids their kids won't find out about sex. It's biological, stoopit. Telling kids to just say no to desire and curiosity is like telling a starving person to just say no to hunger. Anyway, don't sweat it. By the time they're grown you will have so scared, confused, and Sissified them that they won't want to have real sex anymore.

And as for the hypersexuality of hip-hop videos, it should be obvious that it's merely the flip side of the Sissy sex-as-performance coin. Sissy face on one side, Sissy booty on the other. It's not sex, it's role playing. One side of the coin is all limp, effete fake sex, the other is all vulgar, my-humps-in-your-face fake sex.

Hypersexuality is simply one aspect of the hypermasculinity of the defeated Sissy male. It's all for show. Just as the red state versus blue state "polarization" of our politics is merely a handy myth for the media, the apparent sissy-boy versus bully-boy thing is all on the surface.

On the one side of the scale you have the undeniable fact that a large segment of the American male population has become increasingly soft, effeminate, and passive. In most of our cities, many of our suburbs, and all of our college towns, an awful lot of the males under the age of thirty-five or so are somewhere over on the girly-man side of the scale. The Sissy social engineers have done a great job of declawing and spaying and housebreaking them, of making them more "sensitive," of blunting and blurring their masculinity. They're skinny or fat but always droopy, mopey, gay or gay-ish, their speech all sibilants, their gestures all limp. They're wearing their man-purses over their shoulders and flouncing around in flip-flops. They're the mama's boy, the emo boy, the half-a-gay, the Hardly Boys of *South Park*, the yuppie metrosexual waxing his body and buffing his nails and obsessing more expertly about his fashion labels and teeth whiteners than the most dedicated Valley Girl or JAP shopaholic.

Crowded over on the other side of the scale you find the gangstas, goombahs, jocks, meatheads, skinheads, and gym rats, the high-fiving, beer-drinking, gay-bashing, date-raping, hip-hopping, diamond-toothed phony manly-man guy-guys.

Possible prototypes for the eventual Humans-Humules divide, they're just two sides of the passive-aggressive coin, and neither side does a good job of hiding its crippling insecurity, utter confusion, or dismal ignorance.

And that's why Gameboy loves his guns, real and imagined. In the perpetually adolescent American male, playing with your guns and playing with your dick converge in a way that would've given Freud a raging gun-on. A cigar might sometimes be just a cigar, but a gun in the hand of a Sissy is always a dick. No wonder it's been so hard to get American males to stop playing with them.

There's a reason the words "rape" and "murder" are joined in our culture like the words "salt" and "pepper." Whipping out his dick or whipping out his gun, the Sissy male is trying to make up for a profound lack of confidence in his own masculinity. Gun control is a fine thing, but unless it's backed up by Sissy control it can only be to guns what Prohibition was to drinking. As long as American males are so insecure and confused about their masculinity, they'll be fascinated with guns and violence and general primate macho posturing.

It's this same insecurity that makes the American Sissy such an extraordinarily touchy bastard. It's true that Americans are probably not the touchiest people on the planet right now. That would be certain of your non-American Muslims. But we are touchy bastards for sure. We can't take a joke. We can't stand criticism. In lieu of figuring out how to develop self-respect or do something that actually earns the respect of others, the touchy American Sissy simply *demands* respect and is hypervigilant and hypersensitive about being "disrespected" by others.

Sissy who plays with real guns:

"Are you doggin' me?"

BLAM.

Sissy who plays with play guns:

"Are you insulting me? I'll sue!"

The American Sissy, a Gameboy Named I'll Sue.

American violence comes in three flavors of Sissy:

- The completely safe virtual violence of video games, movies, and TV. This is to actual violence as porn is to sex.
- Domestic violence: American males beating up on American females. Oh yeah, you bad.
- Sissy gangsta kids with semiautomatic weapons standing a block away from one another and pulling the trigger, squirting bullets in all directions. Often the only person they manage to hit is the intended target's pregnant girlfriend, little sister, or grandma on her way to church. Yeah, you *real* bad.

America is not the most violent or gun crazy culture on the planet. Watch fifteen minutes of world news. In fact, gun violence and violent crime in general have been lower lately than at any time in U.S. history. This pretty much kills the widely held idea that continuous exposure to the virtual violence of video games, movies, and TV makes the young American Sissy more prone to violent behavior in life. If that were true, the violent crime rate should be skyrocketing, not declining. There's not much violence in Japan, where the Gameboys are just as obsessed with violent entertainments as we are here. Violent entertainments don't create a fascination with violence in young males. Young male primates are innately prone to violence. Through millions of years of evolution, they've had to fight for their right to party, competing with all other males for food and females. *Counter-Strike* just exploits the urge, the same way Burger King commercials exploit the biological urge to consume fatty calories and *Girls Gone Wild* videos exploit sexual hunger. Blaming Pimp Daddy Productions is just more Sissy infantilism.

But yes, we Americans are still vastly more gun crazy and obsessed with violence than any of those industrialized nations than whom we test lower in math and reading, etc. The homicide rate here is three to four times what it is in those nations. Three out of five of those murders are committed with guns. Imagine the predicament of your average drive-by gangbanger, or any of the nutcases who massacre kids on campuses, if they had to kill people with just a steak knife or their bare hands. If you could do the math, I'd tell you to do the math.

Violent crimes are committed mostly by and against people at the bottom of the economic pile. Drugs and alcohol, those marvelous inhibitors of impulse control, are often contributing factors. You know that guns are the leading cause of death among black teenage males, right? And you *know* all of that adds up to a big reason so many Americans have trouble getting behind strict gun legislation. Their lips say Second Amendment, but their eyes say, "Good riddance. One less drug-addict thug who might rob or rape me someday."

Besides, Americans will never get behind the sort of stringent, universal gun control legislation that would be needed if we really wanted to end gun violence. Americans treat the Second Amendment the way they treat the First: as with freedom of speech, they'd be perfectly happy to take away everyone else's right to own guns, as long as they get to keep theirs. It will never work. Because Average Joe insists on keeping his guns, Crazy Cho gets to have his. With the millions and millions of guns floating around inside Fundadome, it's ludicrous to think that you could keep some of them out of the hands of criminals and crazies, drunks and thugs. As long as we fetishize, eroticize, and mythologize guns, they will be put to the use for which they were intended. If you insist on living in a gun culture, some of you will die as a result of the gun culture.

The only other answer is to go the opposite way, get all NRA and Afghanistan on the problem's ass. *Make bearing arms not just a right but compulsory for all adults.* Make it law that all adult citizens *must* be carrying firearms at all times. Unconcealed, so every other citizen can see them. Link obtaining a gun permit to getting a driver's license. If you get stopped by a cop and he finds you're not packing, he'll hit you with a hefty fine.

What would happen if all the thugs, bullies, gangbangers, terrorist hijackers, angry drunks, and crazies knew that everybody else in the home and on the street, in the 7-Eleven and the plane and the subway car and the classroom was packing? As Robert A. Heinlein wrote, "An armed society is a polite society." He was a science fiction writer, but hey, we're living in a dystopian future now. Maybe we should test it. Already there are many areas of our nation where the idea is in effect being piloted—West Virginia, Arizona, L.A., and Baltimore, to name a few. Baltimore, my hometown, a city of just over 600,000 residents, had 276 homicides in 2006, mostly by guns. An enterprising Mayor's Office once floated a motto, "Baltimore: The City That Reads." Local realists instantly amended that to "The City That Bleeds."

Let's go federal with the program. Outsource the administration to the NRA. Yes, Sissies and Stoopits that we are, we'd screw it all up and the gun-related homicides, suicides, and accidents would go through the roof. But what the hey. There are too many of us anyway. Gaia would approve of thinning the herd. *Guns: it's the green thing to do.* If Al Gore, Arnold Schwarzenegger, and all the tree huggers were really committed to saving the planet, they'd be...Ted Kaczynski.

Failing that, we could reduce at least some gun-related mayhem by reviving the practice of dueling. Dueling fell out of favor in the mid-1800s because Americans had, as we so often do, stoopitized it, reducing it to just another form of murder. But for centuries before that it had been a highly ritualized and controlled venue for men to deal with matters of honor—what we would now call "being disrespected." There were elaborate rules, called the code duello, regulating the who, when, where, how, and why of dueling. There were built-in steps leading up to the duel that gave the offending party plenty of opportunity to issue a formal apology before things got nasty. Since swords and, later, smooth-bore pistols were used, duels were fatal a lot less often than you'd think. Yet honor was always satisfied, for both parties, and the matter was dropped. Also, since the time and the place of fighting were controlled, there was none of the collateral damage we see today when the dissed boyfriend or the drunk thrown out of a dance club shows up later with a Tek-9 and starts spraying rounds all over the place.

With our typical high-mindedness, we look back on dueling as a "barbaric" ritual. As though the drive-by massacre or gunning down your ex-girlfriend's wedding party is more civilized.

There'd be no guns in my movie *Armed * A * Geddon*, no easy Sissy way out. If there were guns the Sissies would stand at either end of the compound, posturing like gangstas, and squirt away at one another until one of them got lucky. B-o-r-i-n-g. No, there'd be only knives, clubs, crowbars, spears, ballpeens. The Sissies would have to get right up on each other and fight like we've fought through almost all of our human and primate existence. It's a very different experience from standing a block away or zipping by in a car and squeezing the trigger. If you've ever been in a real fight, just a drunken brawl even, you know it's nothing like on TV or in the movies or in video games. Real fights are brutal and ugly. The saying "I got my ass kicked" is another Sissy euphemism. In most fights your ass is the *last* thing that gets kicked. Besides, your ass is the one part of your body designed with padding to absorb a kick. That's why those S&K folks are into spanking. You don't see many play-dominants punching their play-submissives in the nose. In a real fight your *face* gets kicked, your skull, your ribs, your guts, your hands, your balls. It hurts like hell. It's very rare for guys to get up after a real fight, dust themselves off, wipe away the decorous drops of blood under their noses, grin and shake hands, and walk off best friends for life. More often, one guy's lying there broken and the other guy is standing over him doing triumphal primate posturing.

It's no reflection on our men and women in uniform that we now fight wars the way we fight among ourselves. It's our culture, and our leaders. In fact, it's a safe bet that no one knows how stoopitly we fight wars now better than the men and women we expect to fight them for us.

Americans knew how to fight wars up through World War II. The principles are basically the same as in a street fight, on a grand scale. The first rule is that if you're going to fight, don't stand around talking about how you're going to fight. Start it and try to end it as quickly and decisively as you can. The second rule is that if you're going to get in it, get in it all the way, and get in it to win. Do whatever you can to be the one doing the primate victory dance at the end.

There is no third rule.

Look at how we fought and ended World War II. We held off getting involved until the Japanese sucker-punched us, but then it was *on*, baby. We showed everyone in the world that we were the world's true, champeen berserkers. We were, and still are, the only nation on the planet berserk enough to nuke our opponents—not once, but twice. The Soviets never nuked anyone. Israel's never nuked anyone. The Indians have not (yet) nuked Pakistan, and vice versa. Even Saddam never nuked anyone. Only the Americans. And that's not even to mention the apocalyptic firestorms we rained on Dresden and Tokyo, in which we melted to death hundreds of thousands of mothers, children, doctors, nuns, schoolteachers, retirees, their dogs, cats, and goldfish.

The message to the world was clear. Fuck with the cowboys, and they'll fuck you up good. Yippie-ki-yay, world. It will be a very, very long time before the Japanese or the Germans get up the stuff to try us again.

That was the last real American war. If we could have stopped the clock in the fall of 1945, America could have basked long in the glory of its finest hour. The History Channel still does. But we barely had a second to enjoy our triumph, because the damn Rooskies insisted on sharing the glory and, more important, the postwar world. Then we went into the Korean War, where we were fought to a bitter and inconclusive standstill by hordes of Asiatics. And then the same in Vietnam. We got our faces kicked by skinny little characters in black PJs who lived on a cup of rice a day. Our manhood has never recovered.

Meanwhile, there was the Cold War. Like the "war on drugs" and the "war on poverty," the Cold War (journalist Walter Lippmann coined the oxymoron—I believe he was also responsible for "soft rock") wasn't really a war in any conventional sense. Lasting roughly forty-five years, it was the longest war Americans never fought. The U.S. and Soviets spent trillions of dollars amassing the most fearsome arsenals ever imagined—and never fired a shot, at least not directly at each other.

You could say that the Cold War was fought entirely in the fevered imaginations of politicians, generals, industry leaders, strategists, journalists—and the billions of civilians who felt threatened, on a daily basis, with annihilation. Fear of an evil enemy is a great motivator of civilian obedience, and politicians both American and Soviet, Republican and Democrat used Cold War paranoia as a way to keep their populaces compliant and conforming. Philosopher Herbert Marcuse suggested in the 1960s that the correct way to picture all those nuclear missiles was not pointing outward at our supposed enemies but pointed *inward*, at each nation's own citizens. He believed the missiles' true purpose was not as weapons of international war, but implements of domestic crowd control. Not spears, but billy clubs.

One of the most fevered imaginations of the era resided inside the head of Herman Kahn. Kahn was the coldest of Cold Warriors, a star theorist and speaker at the RAND Corporation, the air force's think tank for research and development. Kahn was one of the most influential strategists of "nuclear deterrence" and the arms race, the egghead probably most responsible for convincing the leaders of the United States that an all-out nuclear conflict with the Soviets was not only likely but necessary and winnable. His influence could clearly be seen in the nuclear strategizing of John F. Kennedy, who ran for office playing up fears of a "missile gap" and then made the arms race a priority of his administration.

It's easy to see why Kahn was so influential. A self-declared genius and natural showman, he could speak extemporaneously for hours on the purely theoretical ups and downs and ins and outs of thermonuclear destruction. Politicians and generals loved listening, even when Kahn's logic disappeared down a rabbit hole of say-what? pronouncements like "Appropriate arms control could increase the trend toward decreased megatonnage and even toward fewer weapons, but unwise disarmament could set it back."

If that sounds a bit like Dr. Strangelove to you, there's a good reason. Kahn's massive tome *On Thermonuclear War*—a book big enough to kill a Russian just by hitting him with it—inspired Stanley Kubrick's movie *Dr. Strangelove*. Much of the insanely apocalyptic chatter in the film—like the Doomsday Device and discussing the need to choose between "two admittedly regrettable but nevertheless distinguishable postwar environments—one where you got twenty million people killed, and the other where you got a hundred and fifty million people killed"—is almost verbatim Kahn.

After decades of missile-rattling and tough-guy posturing, the Cold War petered out from sheer exhaustion and boredom. It was the first great Sissy war—all talk, theory, and posing. It taught us the disastrous lesson that *we could fight wars without really fighting them*, that not all wars have to be "hot" and brutal and gruesome. Wars could be almost entirely theoretical, fought remote-control from a safe distance, fought by human and technological proxies, and won if you throw a vastly superior force against a pitifully inferior opponent.

The American Sissy and his elected leaders learned these lessons well. We've fought nothing but Sissy wars for a quarter of a century now. Ronald Reagan, our first certifiable Stoopit + Sissy president, an actor who fought World War II in Hollywood, threw the enormous might of the American war machine against...Grenada and Libya. His remote-control lashing out at Libyan women and children, a response to Libyan-backed terrorism, would prove to be a model for later commanders in chief.

His successor George I "won" the Gulf "War" by rolling immeasurably superior forces against a not exactly implacable enemy, an army of terrified conscripts who didn't know who'd kill them first, Uncle Sam or Uncle Saddam. Yeah, we bad. It was also the first truly virtual war, a war fought almost entirely on TV and computer screen, War Beyond Fundadome.

Bill Clinton, the draft-dodging baby boomer, reached into the immense war chest his predecessors had left him and threw handsful of high-tech war toys at...the Balkans and Sudan. Yeah, we *real* bad.

And that brings us to George II and his two Vietnams, massive tragedies for everyone involved. The apotheosis of Stoopit + Sissy, another draft-dodging American male with almost literally no knowledge of the world beyond Fundadome, a yahoo and doofus and trustafundamentalist...oh, why go on. You elected him, stoopit. *Twice.*

Whatever else 9/11 was, it was a gonzo, mad-dog, berserker act of guerrilla warfare and guerrilla theater. *That* was shock and awe, folks, and it succeeded beyond its perpetrators' wildest fantasies.

George II's response was the lashing-out of a bully, a Sissy in tough-guy drag. An utterly predictable, thoroughly unimaginative, carpet-bomb-and-ground-invasion game. It promoted rather than prohibited global terrorism. It mired us, and much of the rest of the world—not that we care much about the rest of the world—in a horrific no-win, all-loss conundrum.

The question, obviously, is not whether we should have responded to 9/11. It's about *how* we responded. There must be ways to go all high-tech and remote-control without also going all Stoopit and Sissy.

In the old days, we would have responded to the gonzo, mad-dog, berserker attack of 9/11 with an even *more* gonzo, mad-dog, berserker retaliation. Here's one scenario.

THE RACE FOR THE KEYS

At noon on 9/11, the president of the United States calls Prince Bandar, the Saudi ambassador, into the Oval Office. The president, sitting behind his desk, addresses the prince, who stands on the American Eagle carpet.

"Prince, fifteen minutes ago I ordered the Pentagon to put the crosshairs on y'all's holy city of Mecca. More precisely, the Kaaba. Now, I want Osama bin Laden's head on a silver platter here in the Oval Office, right here on my desk—looky here, I cleared a spot—by noon tomorrow. If it is not delivered by noon, at noon-o-one we will bomb the Kaaba.

"Now, this will not be your typical nucular bomb. It will be a high-yield neutron bomb. Remember those? My predecessors claimed to have destroyed them all, but we kept a few in storage for moments just like this. This device will detonate in the air directly over the Kaaba, but high enough not to destroy it or much any other architecture. It will, however, rain a massively lethal dose of X-rays over the entire city of Mecca. Many thousands of residents will die within a few hours. The rest will flee. Mecca will be a ghost town in twenty-four hours.

"At that point the Army Corps of Engineers will move in. They will bulldoze the dead into mass graves. Meanwhile, they will collect every key they can find—house keys, car keys, whatever. They will make a great pile of these in the square next to the Kaaba. Israeli Jews will be airlifted into the city, along with some number of poor, starving sub-Saharan Africans. A starting line will be set up at the edge of the square, a starter's gun will sound, and this crowd of Jews and blacks will race to the pile of keys. Each contestant gets to keep as many keys as he or she can grab, and takes immediate possession of whatever building, safe, locker, vehicle, or whatever the keys open. Within three days Mecca, the holiest place in Islam, will be resettled by Jews and Africans.

"Meanwhile, I will still be expecting Osama's head. If you have not delivered it by noon two days from now, a second neutron bomb will be detonated over Riyadh, and the same process will be applied there. On the third day...I dunno. Maybe Cairo, maybe Kabul. My staff is drawing up a eeny meeny list. Every day Osama's head is not delivered, another major city in the Muslim world will be bombed and resettled. And if there's any attempt at retaliation, by anyone within the Muslim world, anyone at all, anywhere, we'll drop one just to show we ain't foolin'...

"Now Prince, your family and mine go back a long ways. My daddy and your daddy shot quail together. I know and you know I know that you can find Osama a hell of a lot faster than I can. And I know you know I mean business. My daddy fought in dubya dubya aye-aye and you know how we ended that one. I am a for-real American berserker cowboy. I will irradiate a hunnerd thousand sand niggers and sleep peacefully that night, then git up and do it again after breakfast. Let a thousand Ground Zeros bloom.

"I want that fella's head on a plaque right up here behind me where every American can see it when I go on TV. So how about instead of standing there with your chin on the eagle's nose you hustle back over to the embassy chop chop and git on the hotline. Bring me the head of Osama bin Laden."

Could the Saudis have persuaded the Taliban to give up bin Laden? If it was that or a Mecca full of Jews, I bet they could. Would they have called our bluff? Depends on how well Bandar understood Americans. *We* would know we're too Sissy to pull off that kind of shock and awe anymore, but would he? Would the Race for the Keys have put an immediate end to terrorism? Probably not, but it's not like we did that anyway, and it would not have gotten us mired in the two simultaneous Vietnams of Afghanistan and Iraq.

But we'd never commit to something like the Race for the Keys anymore. Because for all our bullying, Americans very much want to be seen around the world as *nice guys*. We're the world's Giant Puppy. We want the world to like us, and we want the world to want to be like us. We want to export democracy and the American way from Fundadome to the rest of World World the way we export Big Macs and movies. We yearn for a war we can win and be *liked* for winning, like World War II. There's a reason the History Channel is the Hitler Channel. When we're forced to kick somebody's face in war, we really do want them to pick themselves up, wipe their nose, shake our hand, and become our best fuckin' friend, like the Japs and the Krauts. Abu Ghraib was so upsetting because that's just not how we picture Our American Boys and Girls in Uniform acting. It looked like a cross between a Marilyn Manson video and *Jackass Goes to War*.

Being Sissies, we like to wage war with minimal exposure or danger to ourselves—remote-control, from a great distance, with the highest-tech equipment DoD money can buy. At the same time, being nice guys, we like to keep the collateral damage to a minimum. We like to shoot smart missiles from across the border, or drop smart bombs from bombers so high they're unseen and unheard, yet with the precision to take out the bad guy with the bull's-eye pinned to his chest while leaving the wife and child standing next to him as safe and untouched as we are. As we've Sissified our whole culture, we've lost the heart for cowboy berserker nuke-'em-all warfare.

Thus the Pentagon's ongoing research into and development of "nonlethal weaponry." NLW is designed not to kill the enemy, just make him go away and leave us alone. It's now several generations past the high-powered water cannon and the rubber bullet commonly used to disperse street protests.

The Active Denial System (ADS), for instance, looks like a radar dish, but shoots a directed, invisible heat ray at the enemy. It doesn't injure him, but it does make him hop around like a frog on a hot plate. Presumably this comical sight will be a great morale booster to our troops and relieve some of the stress of battle. Not that the Joint Chiefs asked, but I came up with a few mottoes.

ADS: Hot Plate with an Attitude

ADS: Putting the Fun Back into the Fundamentals of War

Airburst Non-Lethal Munition (ANLM) operates like cluster bombs: a shell opens in midair and rains smaller projectiles. Cluster bombs are really vicious. They tend to leave lots of unexploded ordnance lying around like land mines for innocent civilians to step on or poke with a rake. The Israelis, the true inheritors of our old berserker spirit, love their cluster bombs, and used tens of thousands of them to seed southern Lebanon with lingering death after their ill-conceived invasion in 2006.

ANLM presents a nice-guy alternative. The ANLM shell opens in the air and rains down things like "sting balls" or "point-effect blunt impact" objects—aka "sponge grenades." Sponge grenades! War can't get any nicer-guy than that. The enemy gathers these up, takes them home, and his kids play with them in the tub. Who says we don't know how to win hearts and minds?

In New York City, at about the same time that Bush was invading Afghanistan, we faced another kind of post–9/11 invasion—an invasion of grief counselors. The grief industry is based on the presumption that Americans have grown too stoopit to know how to feel sad without professional instruction, and too out of touch with our emotions and reality to express sorrow without coaching. It's like Method acting for mourners. For this we have no one to blame but ourselves.

The practice of hiring professional mourners for funerals fell into disfavor in this country centuries ago. The grief counselors have revived and therapized it. The instant any tragedy (a widely abused term) strikes, an alarm goes off somewhere in the Grief Center, and squadrons of counselors rush to the victimized (another much abused word) community. It doesn't matter if the tragedy is as general as a hurricane or as particular as a high school kid's dying in a drunk driving accident, the professional vultures descend to feast on the carrion of sorrow, confusion, and shock. And the victims (How proudly we wear that badge of victimhood these days!), who are docile and subservient as always when facing figures of presumed authority and expertise, meekly acquiesce to the professional mourners instructing them in how to grieve, how long to grieve, how to "heal" and how to bring "closure."

Several thousand of these vultures were circling over Manhattan within days of 9/11. Their work done in Columbine, in Oklahoma City, in all those other places stricken by acts of violence or sudden destruction, they flocked to New York City, bringing with them their long do-gooder faces and their pious rhetoric about healing and bereavement and trauma and recovery. Some volunteered their services, others were employed by the not-for-profit and for-profit agencies that make up the industry.

One of these vultures, a professor of religion in Oshkosh, landed in the op-ed page of the *New York Times*, offering the pornographically mawkish argument that since Oklahoma City and New York City had both been sites of terrorist attacks, they were now joined in "A Sisterhood of Grief." The two cities were now members of "'the trauma club.' Both cities are joined at the hip through bereavement." Oklahoma City's "survivors" were supposedly rushing to New York City to help us deal. "Their words will be firm, honest, gentle... They will help those wounded in mind, body and spirit..."

Oh my God, what hideous grief-counselor palaver. You can almost see the author in his deacon's weeds, wringing his bony hands and crying big crocodile tears of phony sympathy.

Yet Professor Grief had a beef with us New Yorkers: we were in an unseemly rush to heal ourselves.

Professor Grief declared it "astonishing and painful" to hear New Yorkers say they were ready to move on and put the grieving behind them. "What disrespect for the enormity of the event," he moaned. "Before there is any talk of healing, there must be reflection, an awe-filled accounting of what was lost."

Actually, what was astonishing, and enraging, was this self-appointed umpire of Good Grief accusing New Yorkers of disrespect because of the way we were dealing with the aftermath of 9/11. New Yorkers had in fact shown *tremendous* respect for the enormity of the event, and for all its victims, and for all those involved in rescue and recovery efforts. We'd been grieving in our own way, holding our funerals and memorial services and concerts, volunteering to overcapacity and raising millions of dollars in aid. What an insult to have some Hickville academic tell us we were not grieving the right way, like the good survivors of Oklahoma City.

You know who know how to mourn? Jews know how to mourn. They put the dead in the ground right away, then sit shiva. For seven days relatives and friends gather at the deceased person's home to lend the bereaved an ear or a shoulder to cry on. You're allowed to grieve as loudly and intensely as you feel like, for seven days. But when this mourning period is over, everyone is expected to get back to their lives, to move on. Death is inevitable, but life is for living. Get on with it.

The rest of America should learn how to sit shiva. When something bad happens—a death in the family, a devastating flood, a plane crash, a terrorist attack, a heartbreak, whatever it is—give yourself a week to grieve, as deeply and loudly and bitterly and inconsolably as you must.

Let it all out. Exhaust yourself with grief. You don't need a professional to tell you how you "should" be feeling or acting. Just do it. And at the end of the week get on with your life.

But the American Sissy loves grief. We adore "tragedy"—if not our own, then anyone else's. There's nothing we enjoy more than mourning by proxy over other people's misfortune. We have a morbid, mawkish fascination with sorrow. We love to sit at the TV and "share" the grief of others. When 9/11 happened, when Hurricane Katrina struck, many millions of Americans sat glued to their TVs and "shared" the sorrow of the "victims."

Is that because TV connects us all and makes us more empathetic? Maybe. A little. But what's really going on isn't empathy, it's envy. We envy other people's disasters and misfortunes, because that makes them victims. And *in America today there's no higher moral or social status one can attain than victimhood.* Sissy culture is a victim culture. We honor our victims at least as much as we do our heroes. We make saints and martyrs of them, when all they were—and this is certainly sad enough—was people going about their daily routines at home or at work or at school. We elevate them and their families to faux-celebrity status. It's the *American Idol* of victimhood.

The 9/11 victims' families were rewarded with large cash gifts, nonstop and respectful media coverage—except from a few conservative skeptics such as Ann Coulter and Glenn Beck—and extraordinary political power to influence everything from the construction plans for the new World Trade Center to the congressional 9/11 hearings. Coulter was doing her usual over-the-top schtick when she maligned the so-called Jersey Girls, the four most vocal and visible 9/11 widows, as camera-loving "harpies," but there was justification for her being so fed up with them. The fact that their spouses worked at the WTC and yours didn't doesn't make those women or their opinions more important than yours. Yes, they are victims of 9/11. Aren't we all, in one way or another. Aren't a whole lot of other people in the world now, as the combatants on both sides in the War on Terror lash out like bullies.

You want some grief counseling? Here's some: Get over yourselves.

But Sissies don't need professional help to deal only with grief. We need professional help to deal with *life*.

What are you on lately? Zoloft, Effexor, or Paxil? What about your kid? Is it Ritalin or Adderall?

We all know that Sissies are now way overmedicating themselves, so let's make this brief.

For a short while in the 1970s I worked as a nurse's aide on a locked ward of a mental institution. It was a grim, old-fashioned, state-run Bedlam, basically a prison for psychotics. The guys on the ward were schizophrenics, failed suicides, self-mutilators, self-abusers—a can of assorted nuts, as one of the experienced nurse's aides said to me my first day.

One guy got up every morning, stripped the sheets from his bed and several others, and stuffed them down his pajama pants. He waddled around all day like he was wearing an inner tube inside his pants. He said it was protection against "the morphodytes," who he feared would cut off his penis and stuff it in his mouth. At some point every afternoon another guy, known as Monkey Boy, would climb the steel grate that barred the windows in the dayroom. He'd hang up near the ceiling and make woo-woo noises, disturbing the rest of the patients as they stared at the TV. We had to poke him with brooms to get him down. Another guy took frequent "air showers." When the ventilator in the ceiling went on, he'd stand under it and go through all the motions of showering. He said it was the only clean air in the building. He was right. Another guy had terrible rage control, but tried not to hurt others when he flew into one of his fits. His arms were covered with crescent-shaped teeth marks where he'd bitten himself rather than attack others.

Twice a day, every day, these guys lined up for their meds. These guys sorely needed their meds. When they went off their meds, they went very crazy.

Not long after I worked there, America decided it was more humane to have these guys wandering the streets than pacing the dayroom. The doors of all those old-school mental asylums were thrown open. It was like the entire nation was doing an amateur production of *Marat/Sade*. I was once standing in the checkout line of a grocery store when there was a big commotion up ahead. It was the self-biter, now free to walk the streets. He'd exploded into one of his screaming jags and was throwing cans of peas and rolls of paper towels at the terrified checkout lady. It was near the end of the month, and I figured he must have run through his meds.

All those drugs followed those people out of the asylums and into the mainstream. Sissies *hate* it when we see someone else has something we don't. It doesn't matter what it is—money, fame, tragedy, insanity—if somebody else has it, we think we're being disrespected if we don't get some of it, too.

So we all got us some psychoactive drugs. Sissy America is now by far the most medicated society on the planet. We've turned the whole country into an asylum. You've seen the statistics. Between 1998 and 2002 alone, sales of antidepressants went up 73 percent, and Ritalin and Adderall shot up 167 percent. Something like 6 million kids are now on ADD/ADHD drugs. Prescriptions of those drugs for children *aged two to four* rose by half during the 1990s. *The fastest-growing market for sales of antidepressants now is preschoolers.*

Beats me what preschoolers have to be so depressed about, unless it's their weight problems and knowing they'll probably get diabetes before they get their driver's licenses.

Next time a fat three-year-old drug addict holds you up at an ATM, don't come crying to me, Sissy.

We are now taking prescription meds—or giving them to our kids—for sadness, shyness, restlessness, sleeplessness, boredom, lousy eating habits, and, of course, to get the erections we're too drugged-out, fat, and lazy to have without help.

Funny, we all know we're drug addicts, but if you ask any of us we always say, "Oh no, me and my kid need them. We've been *diagnosed*. It's those other people."

And then we blame the FDA and the drug companies. Who are surely our enablers, just as our doctors are all dealers and pushers. But *we* are the addicts, and all these meds are just one more way we hide from reality here inside Fundadome.

Boy, when those lean and hungry barbarians show up and start eating us, they're in for a lot more than an MSG rush.

The Cold War Sissified more than the way we fight wars. It also conditioned us to live in a constant state of fear and anxiety, to worry all the time about some threat or attack, to be on alert for enemies foreign or homegrown. For a good three decades we were told we were threatened with mutual assured destruction—MAD, one of the all-time great acronyms.

The threat of MAD gave rise to a peace activists' group, SAD—Sissies Against Destruction. For several years they sought out every one of those round, yellow-and-black air-raid shelter signs they could find and pasted them over with their famous logo, the round, yellow-and-black SAD Face. At some point in the 1970s some enterprising optimist turned that frown upside down and created the Happy Face. But by then the membership of SAD had disbanded, become hippies, and gone off to the farm, where some can still be found today, grizzled and graybearded, boring their skate-punk grandchildren with their tales of mythical beasts like Tricky Dick, who did something something with something called the Gold Water.

By the time the daily threat of nuclear annihilation faded into the background, we'd become such Sissies, so used to feeling threatened all the time, that we began to fill in with a long list of other "threats" to worry or panic about. Many of them played on our Sissy dread of disease and our own mortality—not to mention our fear of direct contact with others—by scaring us with threats of some kind of *infection*. In 1976, the Centers for Disease Control threw the entire nation into a mass panic about swine flu, after a single soldier at Fort Dix died of it. President Gerald Ford, dutifully citing the Great Influenza Pandemic of 1918—a *real* epidemic that killed at least 50 million people worldwide, including more than half a million Americans—declared that every man, woman, and child in the United States must be inoculated immediately. Millions of dollars' worth of vaccine was hastily prepared and rushed out, and worried Sissies stood in long lines to get their shots.

Fifty million Americans had been inoculated when the program was abruptly halted, because it turned out that the vaccine had caused paralysis in a number of people, killing some of them. Swine flu didn't kill and maim them—Sissy panic did. In fact, the *only* American who died of swine flu that year was that poor soldier. A deluge of lawsuits rained down on the CDC, and the agency's reputation was severely damaged.

You might think that such a colossal embarrassment would make the CDC and other health agencies a little more cautious about rushing to judgment on nonexistent epidemics in the future. Instead, just the opposite happened. It's like they're in a race to find a new disease and then run to the TV cameras to shriek at us Sissies about it. Desperate to prove their value as our vigilant defenders against disease, health agencies scour the globe to find any evidence of a new possible epidemic they can announce to the world, scare us all about, and then miraculously defeat. Our heroes! Thank you for defending us from...what was it again? Chinese chicken flu?

In the '80s it was, of course, AIDS, and the CDC and all media screaming at us that we were all gonna die. Not just the specific populations the epidemic seemed to be targeting, but all of us. We went to bed having a Sexual Revolution and woke up to see WAR IS OVER–size headlines shouting SEX = DEATH. People were terrified not only of sex but of touching anyone who might be gay or "infected." Going to or working in a hospital was a death sentence, and forget about going to the dentist.

Using a public restroom was suddenly not merely a mildly distasteful experience, but lethal. Daily newspapers ran front-page charts predicting the rapid spread of the epidemic. They looked like Apple's stock chart after the debut of the iPod. As late as 1988, the respected sex researchers Masters and Johnson were still warning of an impending heterosexual AIDS epidemic in their book with the classically Sissy scare title *Crisis*. If AIDS had spread the way they all shrieked at us it would, there would have been no American Sissies left alive to panic about Y2K at the millennium.

Remember Ebola? No, you probably don't. The appearance of this virus in Central Africa in 1994 was trumpeted as another great plague that would sweep the planet; best-selling books and even a movie helped spread the panic. Ebola abruptly dropped out of the media after killing all of 244 people, all of them in Central Africa. Those deaths were sad, but they didn't add up to a world plague. And they were nothing compared to the hundreds of thousands of Africans who died that year of dysentery, TB, and other diseases that are too common and boring to write books and movies about.

After the 9/11 attacks traumatized the nation, we might have looked to the government and media to calm our fears. Instead, they went into overdrive to make us *more* fearful and keep us in a state of high anxiety.

Starting just one week after 9/11, a handful of envelopes filled with anthrax spores were mailed to a few politicians, TV stations, and newspaper offices. Many more envelopes filled with harmless white powders were sent as malicious hoaxes to other political and media outlets, including the paper where I was the editor. Happily, I was in the bar across the street when our receptionist opened the envelope and plotzed. Someone called 911. Guys in full HAZMAT gear arrived to seal our office, look through our mail, and totally disrupt business.

The anthrax panic made Sissies around the country afraid to open their phone bill or shake their postal worker's hand. When the fog of terror passed in a couple of months, it turned out that a whopping twenty-two people had been infected, and five died.

After anthrax, American Sissies were afraid to go out of their homes in the summer of 2002 for fear of being bitten by a mosquito carrying the West Nile virus. By the end of the summer, only six hundred cases of West Nile fever had been reported nationwide, with thirty-one fatalities. That was sad, but it wasn't an epidemic worthy of mass panic. There were roughly eighty gun fatalities in America *every day* during the same period.

That fall, we were told to forget the mosquitoes and panic instead about smallpox, a disease we all thought had been eradicated in the 1940s. Close to 40,000 Americans were vaccinated against it—and then the program was stopped when it was found that the vaccine was causing inflammation of the heart in some recipients. As of 2007, there still have been no cases of smallpox in America since the 1940s.

Despite the fact that neither anthrax nor smallpox nor any other biological or chemical weapons threat had been shown to be anything but theoretical, in 2004 Congress approved the Bush administration's Project BioShield, a $5.6 billion program "to purchase and stockpile vaccines and drugs to fight anthrax, smallpox and other potential agents of bioterror." Over ten years, the government would amass a mighty strategic national stockpile of these vaccines and drugs. In 2006, the *New York Times* reported that Project BioShield was way behind schedule, as government agencies dithered over which drugs to buy, causing major drug companies to give the whole program a pass. That left the field wide open for "relatively small outfits with limited experience. VaxGen, for example, had never taken a drug to market. Its first major product, an AIDS vaccine, flopped in 2003." The company was dropped by NASDAQ in 2004 for accounting errors.

God, I feel so much safer knowing that.

Remember SARS? In 2003, SARS (Severe Acute Respiratory Syndrome) was the new next global plague. It also never happened. SARS caused somewhere around eight hundred fatalities worldwide. Malaria kills more people *every three hours*. No American died of SARS.

The next year came bird flu. Officials estimated in 2004 that as many as 400,000 Americans could be infected. International travel was curtailed to prevent people from tracking bird flu from one nation to another. Chickens were slaughtered in great numbers.

This time, it wasn't just government bureaucrats ratcheting up the fear. People opposed to the government seized on bird flu as a handy weapon to pummel George Bush with. After all, 2004 was an election year. Running for president, John Kerry accused the Bush administration of not doing enough to develop and stockpile the required vaccine to save America from the coming epidemic. Ralph Nader added his dire warnings that "the Big One," as he called it, was imminent. Liberal journalist Mike Davis wrote a whole book about our government's lack of preparedness for the coming apocalypse, called *The Monster at Our Door*. Way to work our infantile imaginations, Mike. Why didn't you go ahead and call it *Look Out, Sissies, It's the Giant Sick Chicken Monster!*?

As of August 2006, the World Health Organization estimated that a total of *138* people had died worldwide from bird flu. That's 399,862 fewer than the predictions for the U.S. alone. What percentage is 138 out of the 6.6 billion people on this planet? My calculator can't do the math.

But I don't need the calculator to know that this was no Great Influenza Pandemic.

I don't know that you'd want to draw any direct parallel, but it is awfully interesting that a similar panic about *infection* helped motivate Germans to isolate and exterminate 6 million Jews in the 1930s and '40s. Jews were believed to be a public health problem. It was said that Jews, by their very presence, spread typhus and other contagious diseases. Schoolkids were marched through exhibitions that compared Jews to rats, lice, and germs. Removing Jews from the healthy German body politic and then eradicating them was seen, James M. Glass writes in *"Life Unworthy of Life,"* as "a problem in sanitation management."

Think about that—the Holocaust as a public health scare. Jews, the SARS of the 1930s. A panic whipped up not just by Goebbels's loony Nazi propaganda machine, but also by supposedly sane, humane German health care workers and medical scientists.

I always knew the Nazis were Sissies. You can tell from all that S&K gear they wore. Nazissies.

One of Osama bin Laden's signal achievements on 9/11 was to help nostalgic boomer Bush and his neocon staff bring back Cold War paranoia, big time. One of President Bush's first acts on September 11, 2001, was to resuscitate the Cold War Continuity of Government (COG) program to safeguard key members of the federal government in time of nuclear attack by the Soviets. (Notice that he thought of the safety of himself and his cronies first, the Sissy. Too bad he didn't move so quick to safeguard the health of Ground Zero workers and neighbors.) Under this plan the federal government, beginning in the Eisenhower years, dug a system of up to a hundred underground bomb and fallout shelters under and around Washington, D.C., in a wide arc from Site R, a large bunker in Pennsylvania just across the state line from Camp David in Maryland, down through the mountains of Virginia and West Virginia as far south as North Carolina.

Key members of government—from the White House to Congress to the FCC and so on and so on—had designated "emergency command and relocation" bunkers they were to go to in case of imminent attack. In those bunkers, protected behind steel blast doors and walls of reinforced concrete, they would wait out a nuclear war with the Rooskies, eating army rations and flipping through last month's magazines until the fallout had settled and they could emerge to run the country again. What was left of the country, anyway.

When the Cold War ended in the 1990s, worrying about COG slid to a back burner. Some bunkers, including Site R and Mount Weather in Virginia, were maintained on a low-readiness, semisecret status. Others were decommissioned, like the Mount Pony bunker outside Culpeper, Virginia, where the Federal Reserve had stockpiled billions of dollars in cash to be used to prime the pump of a post-nuke national economy. One even became a well-known tourist attraction—Project Greek Island, a vast complex hidden underground at the very swank Greenbrier resort in the West Virginia mountains. It was meant for all members of Congress and their aides. President Eisenhower chose the Greenbrier because he liked to golf there with Sam Snead. After the bunker was decommissioned in the early 1990s, the Greenbrier turned it into a tourist site. Of course.

I took the tour in 2006. It began at a giant nuclear blast door sealing a tunnel bored into a hillside under the vast plantation-style hotel. The bunker exuded all the charm of an underground parking garage. The tour proceeded down a long, echoing corridor of gray concrete to what would have been the distinguished guests' first stop: the decontamination area. There they would have been stripped, blasted by high-powered shower nozzles, and handed identical olive-drab military fatigues.

The rest of the place was no more uplifting to the spirit. Eighteen dormitory rooms were once filled with narrow bunk beds and lockers. For meals, freeze-dried MREs (Meals Ready to Eat, the military's version of Swanson TV dinners) would be doled out in a bright but cheerless cafeteria. Narrow corridors with linoleum floors under buzzing fluorescent lights connected stuffy, windowless rooms.

Thoughts of Dr. Strangelove came easily and often along the tour. In a briefing room, the legislators could stand in front of murals of either the Capitol dome or the White House to televise messages to their constituents, should any be alive and have electrical power. Two bleak halls that resembled high school auditoriums would have served as Senate and House chambers. Small lounge areas looked like the waiting rooms in dentists' offices.

The bunker was built to shelter the politicians and their aides, but not their families, who would have had to fend for themselves with all the rest of us Sissies. I tried to imagine Lyndon Johnson, Sam Rayburn, Tip O'Neill, and Mike Mansfield prowling the dismal halls in their matching olive-drab uniforms, contemplating the fate of their loved ones above. Not surprisingly, the bunker infirmary was well stocked with antidepressants.

The Greenbrier's resident historian told me that when the bunker was first opened for tours in the '90s it seemed a morbid relic of Cold War paranoia. It had been a long time since Americans seriously contemplated being attacked on their own soil. Since 9/11, though, visitors found it harder to maintain a bemused detachment.

"It sounds perverse to say it, but 9/11 was good for business," was how he put it.

And how. With 9/11, the Bush administration kick-started the COG program back to high-alert status. In March 2002, the *Washington Post* revealed that Bush had designated a "shadow government" of perhaps a hundred senior members of the executive branch who had started doing regular tours of duty in various Cold War–era bunkers in and around D.C. The idea, just as in Eisenhower's days, was that if terrorists detonated some kind of nuclear device or dirty bomb in D.C., a skeleton crew of the executive branch would be safe and sound underground. Reputedly, Vice President Cheney's frequent and mysterious absences from public view after 9/11 coincided with his "bunker duty," possibly at Mount Weather or Site R.

The president was far from the only American Sissy who welcomed the return of the Cold War. "Survivalism," a preoccupation of right-wing conspiracy kooks in the 1990s—Timothy McVeigh was one—went mainstream in the 2000s. It started with Sissies hoarding bottled water and flashlight batteries during the hilariously stoopit Y2K panic, but it spread a lot more widely over the next few years as Sissies panicked about terrorist attacks, super-hurricanes, and power-grid failures. All sorts of Web sites cropped up offering to sell you survival guides and survival kits. A typical product, the Quake Kare 4 Person Deluxe Survival Kit, included nutrition bars, water purification tablets, a tent, a radio and flashlight, toilet bags, and, of course, a Swiss Army knife. Survival kits for your Sissy pets sold separately. The normally staid *Slate* even started a regular column, "The Survivalist."

Temporary shelters were also selling. That's interesting, because Americans never really got with the build-your-own-bomb-shelter idea back in the 1950s and '60s. Some folks outfitted their basements or storm cellars for nuclear holocaust, but most folks figured, rightly, that if their government got them into a shootin' match with the Rooskies, it was the government's job to provide adequate shelter. Unfortunately, this went against the instincts of the notoriously stingy Eisenhower, who saw to it that plenty of those bunkers were built for his key government workers, but refused to spend the enormous bucks it would cost to safeguard the rest of the population. Instead, the government spent far less to produce training films and other public disinformation programs to convince Americans that in case of nuclear war all we had to do was "duck and cover" under our school desks or dining room tables, wait for the blast with our faces covered, and then stand up and go back about our business in the new post-nuke world. I can remember us learning how to scoot under our desks in elementary school. Like that was gonna do us any good. The standard joke was that while we were down there we should kiss our asses good-bye.

By the way, you know who has the most nuclear shelters per capita in the world? The Swiss. Switzerland has shelter for virtually every citizen. No doubt well stocked with Swiss Army knives. Rod Serling could have done a *Twilight Zone* about it. An astronaut comes back after a long mission to find that there's been global nuclear war. The only people who survived were the Swiss. The whole planet is now inhabited by people wearing lederhosen and building cuckoo clocks. Switzerland has expanded to become Switzerworld.

The Cold War, Part Deux, brought the American Sissy's paranoias about strangers, outsiders, and Others from a back burner to the front, and turned up the heat from a simmer to a high boil of mass panic, called Homeland Security. In addition to turning our society inside out and upside down over raghead terrorist atomikazes, there's a renewed focus on that other species of Other, the little brown illegal immigrants flooding across our naively naked and unprotected southwestern borders.

Typically, our simple and stoopit answer to this is to construct a Really High Wall, aka the Great Wall of Mexico, along the 2,000-mile border. It won't work. Mexicans know how to use ladders. They use them all the time to trim our trees, pick our apples, and clean out our gutters. If you build the wall fifteen feet high, they'll bring sixteen-foot ladders. They're Mexicans, not Stoopit Americans.

I have a better idea. In the 1920s, the original War on Drugs focused on pot. Like all subsequent wars on drugs, the 1920s version had an ulterior motive: it was really a War on Mexican Immigrants, who even then were pouring across the border, scaring the hell out of Texas cowboys and taking away the slave-wage fruit-picking jobs from the honest, hardworking white folks in Orange County. The feds used pot panic as an excuse to round up Mexican immigrants en masse and ship them back where they vamoosed from.

I think this idea should be revived. If Mexicans really are all potheads, instead of constructing a border wall of steel and concrete, we should create a human wall:

The Wall of Dealers

Round up all the pot dealers in the country and line them up along the border, with sacks of highest-grade marijuana (grown on federally subsidized corporate farms) at their feet. Offer every illegal Mexican immigrant in the country a kilo of kind bud if s/he goes back to Mexico.

Problem solved. God knows who will be left to blow our leaves around and raise our kids, but we can deal with that next.

The Wall of Dealers would have an added benefit of prompting the voluntary relocation of large numbers of American slackers and potheads to Chihuahua and Sonora and Baja, where they can annoy our little brown neighbors with their stoned blabbering and ceaseless Hacky Sack play. If Mexicans get the impression that the stoners are representative of all America, they will be far less inclined to sneak over here.

I know, I know. *Nemo propheta in patria.* I get that a lot.

The Cold War also switched on a love-hate relationship with the Apocalypse that has lain dormant in American culture all along, and periodically rises to the surface. We're fascinated by the idea of Armageddon, the End of the World, the Final Conflict. "Ah screw it, let's just blow it all up and start over" appeals to our fatalism and defeatism, while the romance of being the Last Man on Earth tickles our infantile narcissism. It's also the last resort of Stoopits, who can't figure out how to fix the mess we've made and just wait for God to step in and clean it all up for us. Who knew God was Mexican?

This obsession with The End shows up most obviously in our homegrown cults and religions, from the Adventists and Jehovah's Witnesses to Jim Jones and Heaven's Gate. But it's all over our mythology, our media, and our entertainment and our Sissy politics is shot through with it. There's that delicious, spine-tingling thrill of apocalyptic dread you get when you hear about terrorist atomikazes blowing us all up with their suitcase nukes and "dirty bombs." (What a wonderfully Freudian term that is. Ooo, a *dirty* bomb. A *naughty* bomb. A nasty, dirty, poo-poo caca bomb.) Or when you watch extreme weather porn and see those tsunamis, hurricanes, twisters, volcanoes, and earthquakes unleash their biblical wrath on matchstick cities, towns, villages, and, of course, trailer parks. (Now *there's* something that should be banned, along with guns: mobile homes. They're not homes, they're homing beacons for tornadoes.) TV weather people positively vibrate with preorgasmic excitement when the weather turns really, really Surrender Dorothy.

And obviously global warming is an apocalyptic secular religion. Gaia's Witnesses.

We *love* scaring ourselves with this stuff. It's the greatest ghost story of all time. Gaia the Ghost.

By the 1970s the general level of Sissy anxiety was so well established that it took no effort for our rumormongering media to whip what were little more than urban legends into full-on nationwide blind Sissy panics. The razor-blades-in-apples legend almost killed Halloween. A few bottles of poisoned aspirin in and around Chicago prompted the obsession with tamper-proof packaging that now makes opening a bottle of aspirin such a headache. This blossomed into the mania for hermetically sealing every product from apples to Apples in bombproof, *very* Gaia-unfriendly plastic, and for sticking warning labels on every single surface inside Fundadome. Listen, if you're such a Stoopit you need a warning label to tell you not to blow-dry your hair while taking a bath, you're too stoopit to (a) read the label and (b) live.

A decade ago, a guy I knew tickled me by wondering when bowling balls were going to come with stickers that said

WARNING: FOR EXTERNAL USE ONLY

I haven't been bowling in a while, but I suspect that's happened by now.

A few scary tales about hitchhikers was all it took to kill that time-honored mode of cheap transportation, one that had brought millions of strangers together for brief periods of good old American how-do-where-ya-headed? camaraderie over many years. The kids-on-milk-cartons campaigns of the '80s ensured that millions of Americans imbibed a morbid dread of strangers along with their Wheaties and coffee every morning. All told the campaign was estimated to have assisted in the return of something under 1,500 "missing" children, the vast majority of whom proved to be either runaways or kids spirited off by one parent from the other. The absurd Y2K flapdoodle at least had the good grace to vanish at one second past midnight on January 1, 2000, as Sissies everywhere toasted dodging that millennial bullet with a bottle of Poland Spring and some Underwood's Deviled Ham on a Uneeda biscuit.

It would be bad enough if we just sweated these big-ticket disasters and freakish events. But the more Sissy we get, the more we've spread our fears to encompass our entire daily lives. We've become complete food Sissies, afraid of meat, fish, veggies, even peanut butter. We're afraid of the water we drink, the air we breathe, and the ground we stand on. We're afraid of *sunshine*, for fuck's sake.

The British sociologist Frank Furedi, who has written brilliantly about our Sissy culture of fear—without actually using the word "sissy," being a Brit and a sociologist—reminds us that through the darkest days of Cold War paranoia a popular and ubiquitous cartoon character was the bearded, wild-eyed religious fanatic carrying a big sign that said, "Repent! The End Is Near!" He was an extremist, a representative of the "lunatic fringe," a figure of fun. Today, we've all become that guy. His apocalyptic hysteria has migrated from the fringe to the Sissy mainstream. And we're not laughing.

Many of the Americans who lived under the umbrella cloud of the Cold War had already survived the *real* apocalyptic horrors of Dubya Dubya Aye-Aye, and the widespread deprivation and despair of the Great Depression. Many could remember World War I and the Great Influenza Pandemic and other real horror shows. It all gave them a little perspective. Gallows humor is easier if you've actually slipped the noose.

Most American Sissies alive today have known only times of unprecedented peace, prosperity, and security. We're Hobbits. We live longer, safer, more coddled lives than any Americans before us. Those predecessors set it up this way for us, and I suppose we should be grateful to them for it—except that it has undeniably Sissified us. We have lived our lives being stampeded into a panic about one largely theoretical, and often bogus, threat after another. We can't laugh them off so easily, because we have no real-world experiences to compare them with and see how silly and nonthreatening many of these "threats" are.

It's precisely because we're so safe and secure that we're so easily frightened. Citizens of the greatest superpower in the history of mankind, insulated from the big, bad world here inside Fundadome, we're more frightened of the world than ever. A handful of guys armed with box cutters can reduce the mightiest nation in history to cowering Sissitude. Facing few legitimate dangers in our daily lives, we act as though everything were dangerous. Having banished disease and death to the far corners of Fundadome, we're morbidly fascinated with death and wimpily neurotic about our health. Safer than ever, we're obsessively safety-conscious. If you're into risk taking on any level anymore, you're just a Jackass.

Okay, we're not the only Sissies in the world. The Swedes, those Vikings-in-Volvos, are the Sissies of northern Europe. They drive the safest cars in the world, on the safest highways, ride the safest bikes, inhabit the safest houses, and have the lowest accident rate in the industrialized world. And still they obsess about making it safer. One Stockholm psychologist calls Swedes "safety junkies" who are "suffering from a national panic syndrome."

A Danish shrink coined the term "curling parent." Curling is that wacky sport where skaters with brooms manically sweep the ice clean in front of a sliding "curling stone." Shuffleboard On Ice. In slow motion. The shrink used it as a metaphor for the way safety-junkie parents go crazy trying to make life's path safe, clean, and smooth for their kids. He wondered what will happen to those kids when they grow up, leave their parents' overprotective care, and find that life isn't always so smooth and clean and safe and slo-mo.

Some American parents—the eight-year-old single mother, for example—might lack both the wherewithal and the overdeveloped maternal instincts to sissify their kids that way, but the ones who can afford it do. Terrified that their children might come into direct contact with the unclean, unsafe world, they turn them all into Bubble Boy. Not long ago I watched a thirty-something mom pushing one of those VW-size doublewide strollers down a sidewalk in my Brooklyn neighborhood. Twins, the yuppie pro-life twofer. Not only were the kids too big to be pushed around in a stroller—they could have been pushing her—but *they were both wearing those retard-kid bicycle helmets.* To be pushed *in the stroller.* And they did not look retarded.

Now, I suppose there could have been another explanation, but everything about this woman shouted *CURLING MOM!* Her kids are gonna have trouble heading off to Yale if they haven't yet learned how to cross the street. And the other Yalies will make merciless fun of their retard helmets. Unless they're all wearing them by then. Which is a distinct possibility.

For role models of adults who aren't terrified of getting a boo-boo, Kid Sissy can still look to a few of our sports stars—our female sports stars, anyway. Women athletes still throw themselves into whatever sport they're playing with a bravura that makes their male counterparts look like...girls. Women athletes don't have to put their game faces on. Women athletes were evidently born with their game faces on.

As for the guys... Could professional basketball and baseball players get more bratty, whiny, demanding, and ego-bloated? That's not sport, that's an extended temper tantrum thrown by coddled jillionaires. Hockey? It's *Canadian.* Nuff said.

You know who still play real sports? The Irish. We could do worse than to spread Irish football the length and breadth of Sissy Nation. It's the manliest manly sport I've ever watched. It looks like a brutal combination of American football, rugby, bare-knuckle kickboxing, and gang warfare. There's no padding, and no time-outs—if a player goes down, everybody just runs over him. They run constantly, back and forth, back and forth, without pause, except when they slam into each other and go flying ass over charlie into the air. By the second half everybody's bruised and battered and out for blood, and games tend to unravel into donnybrooks in the last ten minutes. But when the final whistle blows, they all head to the nearest pub together. It's glorious mayhem—and I've seen only the way the men play it. There are women's teams too, and I bet they're awesome fierce.

There's also Irish hurling, which bears absolutely no resemblance to curling. Hurling may be an even more berserker sport than Irish football. I suspect the ancient Celts invented hurling to toughen themselves up for battle with the Vikings. It's the barbarian version of lacrosse, wherein two teams of lunatics swinging thick wooden axes run back and forth bashing and tripping one another. Oh yeah, there's a ball involved. It's hard as steel, and they bat it at one another with the speed of a cannon shot. It could take your head off. Spectators spend half the game ducking for cover as wayward shots scream overhead. It's one sport that gives you a workout just watching.

Sadly, it's utterly impossible to picture the average American soccer mom or dad dropping Li'l Sissy or Sis off at hurling practice, and a game of Irish football played by American Sissies would end in tears and lawsuits within the first ten minutes. It's no wonder so many American kids have become grublike lumps of protoplasm permanently affixed to the TV and the Xbox. Their parents have panic attacks every time they step out the door. The old saying that boys will be boys should be revised now: boys will be Bubble Boys.

There have been some pockets of resistance. In 2006, Conn and Hal Iggulden's *The Dangerous Book for Boys* was a best seller in the UK and inspired several knockoffs. A U.S. edition came out in 2007. It was simply a primer that tried to explain to boys how to be boys again. Girls got a chapter, but the wise authors did not engage in any politically correct pretense that boys and girls are identical creatures with the same habits and needs.

It being the twenty-first century, the Igguldens didn't encourage boys to do anything much more "dangerous" than play stickball, throw paper airplanes at each other, and hunt rabbits. But in the twenty-first century even mild activities like those have been forbidden to Bubble Boys by their parents or school administrators, so the book acquired the rebel glow of a subversive manifesto.

It's sad, of course, that we've reached the state where boys need adults to explain to them how to act like boys, but if this book's popularity means a counter-curling-mom revolution is in the offing, maybe we can hope that the next generation of kids will be a little less Sissified.

eanwhile, though, we're still stuck with the hysterical American Sissy, who has become so lazy, so paralyzed with dread, and simultaneously so stoopitized into thinking only in yes-no red state–blue state polarities that his only answers to blind panic are *blind faith*—there's that fundamentalism again—or *idiotic optimism.*

Got problems in your life? Don't bother trying to figure out the solutions. Ask God to work a miracle for you. If your faith is really strong, if you really, really believe, he'll fix it for you.

Got money problems? Play the lottery. Or hit the casino. Better yet, gamble online at the virtual casino. Pray while you play, and God will make you a winner. *Americans now gamble away more money every year than we spend on groceries.* How we've gotten so fat I don't know.

The jumbotronic smash best-selling DVD and book *The Secret*—I almost wrote *The Sissy*—have been engineered and marketed with exquisite precision to appeal to our laziness, our blind faith, our idiotic optimism and infantilism. *The Secret*—and all the other "law of attraction" schemes out there—simply takes Norman Vincent Peale's 1952 *The Power of Positive Thinking* and Sissifies, simplifies, and stoopitizes it for the twenty-first-century American. The message itself is unchanged. Whatever you want—money, love, health, happiness—if you think positive thoughts about it, you will attract it to you. And if you think negative thoughts—"Damn, how am I gonna pay all these bills?" or "Oh my god, lung cancer!"—you'll just attract more bills or more illness. You are explicitly instructed not to worry or work too hard, because that will generate more negativity. Don't worry, be happy, think good thoughts and click your heels, and that BMW will magically appear in your garage, your cancer will vanish, your dream lover will ring the doorbell.

If you think I'm exaggerating, you're the last American alive who did not read the book, watch the DVD, or see Oprah shilling for this stuff.

Peale, who came from a Methodist background, turned the old-fashioned Protestant work ethic inside out. Previously, God had been like a stern but fair boss of the cosmic factory, and we were all his employees. If we worked diligently, honestly, and faithfully, God would pay us a fair wage in this world, with an extremely generous retirement package in the next. Peale turned that around and said God worked for us—he actually called God the "slave" of our desires. All we had to do was pray and think good thoughts about what we wanted, and God would obediently deliver. Just like *I Dream of Jeannie*, though not as sexy.

Fifty-odd years later, *The Secret* has updated that idea by turning "God" into the more New Age-y "Universe" and given it a new consumerist, home-shopping spin. The Universe is not your slave but "your catalogue. You flip through it and say, 'I'd like to have this experience and I'd like to have that product and I'd like to have a person like that.' It is You placing your order with the Universe. It's really that easy." Never mind that flipping through catalogues and ordering whatever we want is how we've amassed roughly *two trillion dollars* in credit card debt. If you make one of your purchases a copy of *The Secret*, you'll learn how to make those credit card bills magically disappear.

The Secret works our infantilism, taking the New Age idea of "visualization" and stoopitizing it into the instruction, "Be like a child, and make-believe." If you make-believe that you're rich or happily married or on a world cruise, it will come true. Peale called this self-hypnosis and talked a lot of Freudianism about the conscious and unconscious, but a half century later that's all too complicated and uses too many big words. All American Sissies know how to make-believe, however. We go through most of our lives here inside Fundadome making-believe.

The Secret also appeals, with an appalling Happy Face cynicism, to our sense of futility and fatalism about all the "negative" things in the world such as poverty, hunger, and war. It basically blames the victims, saying that people ravaged by war or famine somehow must have attracted that negativity to them. If you worry too much about these things, feel too bad for those people, you'll only be generating more negativity for them, and for yourself. *The Secret* suggests that you stop paying attention to the news, since so much news is bad news. Just concentrate on making-believe that the world is a safe and happy place, free of hunger and war and injustice, and the Universal Genie will grant your wish.

You can see the devolution of America here in three easy steps:

- from Protestant Work Ethic to
- Pseudo-Protestant Get-Rich-Quick-'N'-Easy scheme to
- Nondenominational Consumerist Sissy Get-Rich-Quick-'N'-Easy scheme

The Secret isn't positive thinking, it's *wishful* thinking. Primitive, magical thinking. Lucky horseshoe over the door superstitious not-thinking. Wish for it, whine for it, what's the dif. Is there any question why this thing has been a megazilla best seller?

There's a big difference between a *positive attitude* and *idiotic optimism*. Rutgers sociologist Karen A. Cerulo analyzed our idiotic optimism in her 2006 book *Never Saw It Coming*. Evidently, humans (not just Americans) find it much easier to envision a rosy, happy future than to anticipate and plan for the worst-case scenario. Cerulo offers dozens and dozens of examples, from parents who see their babies having developmental problems and simply hope they'll grow out of them to aging baby boomers like me who make absolutely no provisions for their senior years. We even stumble like Happy Wanderers into the grave, the one guaranteed worst-case scenario in the world. Few Americans make wills or any other kinds of provisions for this sure thing. But three out of four Americans believe in life after death.

When individuals organize in groups—corporations, government, the military, or just a gaggle of friends out for a lark—we're even more prone to stray blindly into dumbass disastrous situations. It's like the Stoopit areas of our brains all vibrate in synch. Sociologists have identified various types of Stoopit group behavior, including groupthink, the "risky shift," and "systematic stupidity."

Groupthink is more pernicious in a way than mass hysteria, because it involves *a conscious decision to do the stoopit thing.* William H. Whyte Jr., who coined the term in the early 1950s, explained, "We are not talking about mere instinctive conformity—it is, after all, a perennial failing of mankind. What we are talking about is a *rationalized* conformity—an open, articulate philosophy which holds that group values are not only expedient but right and good as well." (Emphasis added.)

Taking up Whyte's thread twenty years later, social psychologist Irving Janis focused his *Victims of Groupthink* (1972) on the "mindless conformity and collective misjudgment" that occur "in a clubby atmosphere of relaxed conviviality." He defined groupthink as "a deterioration of mental efficiency, reality testing, and moral judgment that results from in-group pressure." That is, groupthink = stoopitization.

For his examples Janis selected what were then more or less recent fiascoes in American foreign policy: the FDR administration's failure to see Pearl Harbor coming, the JFK administration's foolish Bay of Pigs adventure, and others. Anyone can easily think of more recent instances. Janis described how a president and his inner circle of friends and advisers can all agree to agree on the stoopitest idea or course of action, choosing to ignore mountains of contrary evidence. Behind closed doors in their inner sanctum, a "concurrence-seeking tendency" takes over.

Janis argued that it's not a case of yes-men nodding their heads in unison at whatever the boss says. It's more an in-crowd psychology, in which an elite group of like-minded individuals convince themselves of their group's intellectual and moral superiority, so that whatever decision they reach, no matter how stoopit it is on the surface, *must* be the right one because *they* made it.

Once a consensus is reached, any criticism of the group decision is received as a criticism of the group itself. So members circle their wagons, not only insulating themselves from outside critics "who threaten to disrupt the unity and esprit de corps of their group," but also pressuring any member who has lingering doubts to keep them to himself. To express doubt openly is to be seen as a disruptive element, not a team player, and risk banishment from the power circle. Loyalty to the group is prized more highly than being correct, even if it becomes evident later that the group has made a disastrous decision. In fact, that's when loyalty and "staying the course" are most expected.

Group thinking doesn't always lead to groupthink. After the Bay of Pigs, President Kennedy changed his decision-making process, encouraging candor and dissent among his close advisers, and opening the inner circle to the counsel of outsiders. That's how he developed the more carefully nuanced response to the Cuban missile crisis.

Not all presidents since Kennedy have benefited from his example. The foreign policy decisions made by the George W. Bush administration yield numerous textbook examples of groupthink. Bob Woodward's *State of Denial*, a detailed account of the in-group decision making on the war in Iraq, is more than five hundred pages of stoopit groupthink in action.

Groupthink is not confined to politics, obviously. The corporate environment is a hothouse of groupthink. Top corporate management is often an exclusive, chummy club of backslapping howdy-boys, and an increasing number of howdy-girls. Overconfident, insulated, and sharing a sense of in-group invulnerability, they lead their employees, stockholders, and consumers over the edge of the cliff. The recent history of corporate affairs is littered with examples of astoundingly stoopit, and often appallingly unethical and immoral, decisions derived from groupthink. The Enron debacle was only one of the most spectacular.

The risky shift is that moment when the people in a group, facing some obstacle or challenge, all look at one another, grin and shrug, and say, "Oh what the hell, let's go for broke! You only live once!" Quite often, since the Stoopit zones of their brains are all vibrating in synch, they rush into a disastrous, self-destructive course of action. Lemmings probably all experience a risky shift right before running off the cliff together.

"Systematic stupidity" is a term for how small errors of judgment and failures to consider failure can pile up inside an organization to produce gigantic blunders. The *Challenger* disaster is a classic example of smart people making a series of small, independently stoopit, and seemingly insignificant decisions that all linked up in a colossal failure.

What all this means is that, first, we really do bring disaster on ourselves with our foolish choices and terrible planning. Partly it's the result of the sunny-side-up idiotic optimism that can take hold of us when we're joined in a group, a team, happy to be there, proud to be part of it, convinced that what we're doing is the good and right and smart thing, so that any doubt, even a rational concern about some small part of our program, is minimized or banished because it's just not down with the team spirit.

And partly it's because we're so distracted with bogus mass panics about crap like Y2K that we can't think straight about more common risky behavior. Like building our dream home hanging off a cliff with stunning panoramic views of the San Andreas Fault, or plunking our hurricane-magnet mobile homes down in Hurricane Alley. We build the Sunken City of New Orleans in a swamp below the level of the Mighty Mississippi, throw up some dirt levees that will hold if the river rises a little or there's a heavy rainstorm, and it never occurs to us to plan for the sort of really severe weather that occasionally ravages the area. We gather years of intelligence data about terrorist plans to attack inside the U.S. but get caught reading *The Pet Goat* to second-graders on 9/11.

Then, when these bad things do happen—*predictable, even inevitable* bad things such as hurricanes, earthquakes, floods, or simply death—we're shocked, panicked, and hysterical. We react as though *this has never, ever happened before* in the entire history of the universe. And in rush the grief counselors, to help us deal with this "tragic" event, and the preacherman, to explain to us why God lets these bad things happen to good people like us.

When Jerry Falwell said 9/11 was God's punishment on us for being sinful and decadent, a lot of us were outraged. But you know, if there really is a God, and especially if he's the jealous, vengeful Old Testament God preferred by Christians of the Falwell persuasion, might he not have created an Osama bin Laden to punish us? Not for our sinfulness but for our stoopitness, and for imposing on him all the time to give us BMWs and make our cancers magically disappear and save us from tragedies of our own making? If Norman Vincent Peale was right, then God's wrath is a slave revolt. Maybe God's the Nat Turner of the Universe.

Wouldn't *you* be sick of us by now? Is it really just a coincidence that bin Laden looks so much like Satan?

Sissy: "Okay, so far you've ranted about our pampered, lazy, end-of-empire decadence, our fundamentalist mindlock and not-think, our craven consumerist conformism, our confusion about masculinity and sex, our culture of constant anxiety and manufactured panic, and the inherent stoopitness of groups all contributing to our Sissification. Any other factors?"

Me: You bet.

Another huge factor in our Sissification of ourselves was the way we took the goals and achievements of the civil rights and equal rights movements and Sissified and stoopitized them into politically correct victimology and divisive identity politics. The civil rights movement of the 1950s and '60s was a great moment in American culture, forcing us to live up to one of the fundamentals of democracy, the idea that each and every individual has an equal right to life, liberty, and the pursuit of happiness. No kidding, it's right there in the Declaration of Independence. Yes, I am aware that if you've been to college in the past thirty years you were probably trained to shut your eyes and stick your fingers in your ears and go LAH LAH LAH LAH LAH at the mention of those racist capitalist pigs the Foundering Fathers and their hate-speech Declaration of Imperialism and Constipation of the United States and the Bill of Wrong Wrong Wrongs. But you don't even have to read the whole thing. They stuck it in the Preamble, possibly foreseeing the day when university campuses would become fundamentalist mindlock centers.

The civil rights movement started a chain reaction. Seeing

African Americans get their equal rights, a whole lot of other Americans decided that they had an equal right to equal rights: Latino Americans, Asian Americans, American Indians, American women, gay Americans, fat Americans, albino Americans, Americans in wheelchairs, Americans with gray hair, little American people, and so on and so on.

In theory, this was all right and good. Theoretically, all of these types of Americans—okay, most of them—had valid cases to make.

Predictably, though, the proliferation of sometimes dubiously defined identity groups all making demands for equal treatment devolved into a piggies-at-the-trough melee of me-too envy and greed. The demand for equal rights became a competition for *equal shares.* American Sissies saw black Americans getting a slice of the apple pie and whined, "Hey, where's *my* slice?" And then they all crowded around the table, elbowing and jostling and cutting in line. It went from each individual American having an equal shot at *earning* some pie to a gaggle of identity groups and ancestor cults in a contest with one another to claim their place in a pecking order of *victim entitlements* to pie. If I were black, I'd have been right pissed.

"Hey, blacks got a bigger piece of the pie than us. No fair. We First Peoples were victims long before they were."

"Yeah? Women have been victims since the Dawn of (Woe)Man."

"So? I'm a weight-challenged one-legged half-Mexican half-Lumbee HIV-positive transsexual senior homeless illegal alien little person. Beat *that*, girlfriend."

"Oo, snap! But I'm a white heterosexual Christian male. *Everybody* dumps on us."

Reverse discrimination. When it gets that low, when even white guys are demanding a spot in the victim conga line, you know it's the end of the empire and the dawn of the Age of the Sissy.

Victimology, and the middle-class guilt it tapped, lay behind the explosive growth of the monolithic welfare state, which had the hideously undemocratic, un-American effect of trapping poor Americans in a state of permanent infantilized dependency on the public teat. But in the decades of heated arguing about the welfare state, what was often missed was that *all* Americans were becoming infantilized and dependent at the same time. They just suckled on a variety of different teats—a government teat, a corporate teat, a teat that permanently dispensed prescription drugs, a teat from which they could permanently suck escapist fantasies, a teat from which they could drink the milk of fundamentalist not-think, and so on. *The Sissy Nation is not just a welfare state, it's a welfare state of mind.*

Not to get myself confused with those hypocritical fundamentalist Christian Apocalypse–lovin' "We *adore* the Jews!" types, but you do have to note that Jews were the one tribe of Americans who were not elbowing and whining at the victim handout trough, despite the fact that Jews know more about being victimized than all the other victim groups put together. A large subset of Sissies are always complaining that "the Jews run this country." You could do a lot worse, Stoopit.

Before the Sissy Age, to call someone a victim, or to say he had a victim mentality, was not to say something positive about him. Now, a victim mentality has spread all over Fundadome. We honor and reward our victims—victims of criminal activity, victims of natural disaster, people claiming membership in some tribal group Sistorically victimized in their great-great-grannies' days, even people who've become "victims" of the natural processes of life, like aging. Try taking away a senior citizen's "right" to a cheaper ticket at your local multiplex. Just try. You'll be facing a Nuremberg hate-crime trial so fast your head'll spin.

Even in a Sissy culture, though, there are limits. The notion of reparations, of America's paying out some multizillion-dollar lump sum to be divvied up by all who can somehow prove descent from slaves, has been around for years without gaining much traction. That's not because it's preposterous and logistically imponderable. It's because the rest of the Sissies cannot *stand* the idea of black Sissies winning the victim lotto over them.

Then again, if any one tribe of Sissies were paid reparations for their victimhood, they could hardly go on claiming to be victims, could they? Here's an idea:

Universal Victim Reparations

Given that all American Sissies, even straight white guys, are victims now, let's have the government pay *everybody* reparations. One ginormous cash payout. Clean out Fort Knox, rehab it as a Quiznos or Starbucks. Give away every last pfennig the government's got. From that moment on, (a) nobody gets to call himself a victim anymore, and (b) there'll be no more government assistance to anybody, for anything. You got the cash, now use it. If you do stoopit things with it and it doesn't improve your life, that's your problem. In fact, there'll be no more government, period. It'll have bankrupted itself out of operation. Yahoo. A twofer. And then watch how fast the Jews really *do* have all the money and own and run everything.

Or how about this: Instead of focusing on our victimhood and squabbling for handouts, why don't we stop all this negative thinking, be like children, and just make-believe we're all rich, healthy, and happy, in great marriages with wonderful kids and God the Mexican snow-blowing a clear path from the street to our six-BMW garage?

In the Sissies' defense, it's clear that being envious of others for what they have or get is basic to human, and primate, nature. When researchers hand a banana to only one chimp in a group, the rest go, how you say, apeshit.

"Hey, who'd she fuck to get the banana?"

Successful women are only too familiar with this response.

Now multiply those bananas by the billions, and stick little warning-type labels on them that say JOBS, HOUSING, EDU-CATION, CHEAP DRUGS, 10% OFF EARLY BIRD SPECIAL, and suchlike. Start handing them out selectively to those tribes of human primates whom you've designated as qualifying for bananas on the basis of their special protected victim-tribe status. Stand back and watch the monkeys go apeshit.

It's inevitable that a democratic, ostensibly classless and majority-rules society would encourage this type of me-too-want-banana behavior.

From the Founding Fathers onward (shut up, campus Sissies), Americans have debated what we mean by "equality" and the inherent tensions between the principles of individual liberty and equality for all. Libertarians and conservatives usually go so far as to put it "equality *versus* liberty," and frame it as a conflict of socialism versus democracy, the collective versus the individual. There's some justification in that. Equality is horizontal, a collectivist force that seeks to average out people's differences on a flat plane. Liberty is vertical; people stack up according to individual characteristics—status, wealth, skills, personality, achievements, or just dumb luck and happenstance. Some people are at the top of the stack, some in the middle, and some at the bottom. Even people who prefer the horizontal often admit that the vertical is the "natural" order of things. Mashing everybody onto the same horizontal plane requires the application of outside force, some degree of social engineering and grading on a curve.

By stating in the Declaration of Independence that "all men are created equal," the authors—Jefferson, Franklin, John Adams, and two guys named Sherman and Livingston who dropped out of the history books—meant that we all have equal *rights*, which Franklin elsewhere specified as "the enjoying and defending of life and liberty, acquiring, possessing and protecting property, and pursuing and obtaining happiness and safety." They did *not* mean that we are all *the same*, that we all have equal amounts of smarts, strength, talent, ambition, etc.—*or* that it's government's job to ensure that we all have equal money, equal houses, equal jobs, etc. As Adams, the most conservative of the bunch, crankily wrote: "That all men are born to equal rights is true. Every being has a right to his own, as clear, as moral, as sacred, as any other being has... But to teach that all men are born with equal powers and faculties, to equal influence in society, to equal property and advantages through life, is as gross a fraud, as glaring an imposition on the credulity of the people, as ever was practiced."

Touring America some fifty years later, the Frenchman Alexis de Tocqueville fretted about the possibility that a democracy might pervert the principle of equality into just such an obsession with *sameness*, becoming a "democratic despotism" that restricts individuality and individual achievement to ensure that no one is richer, happier, smarter, sexier, taller, faster, stronger, or just plain "better" than everyone else. Such a culture, he reasoned, kills the spark of genius, self-reliance, individual responsibility, ambition, and talent on which a thriving we-the-people democracy depends, and fosters the growth of a paternalistic, social-engineering central government. In *Democracy in America*, published in 1835, Tocqueville was already describing a sort of Sissy fascism that "hinders, compromises, enervates, extinguishes, and finally reduces [the] nation to being nothing more than *a herd of timid and industrious animals of which the government is the shepherd.*" (Emphasis added.)

Kurt Vonnegut began his famous story "Harrison Bergeron," published in 1961, with: "The year was 2081, and everybody was finally equal. They weren't only equal before God and the law. They were equal every which way. Nobody was smarter than anybody else. Nobody was better looking than anybody else. Nobody was stronger or quicker than anybody else." That's because in 2081, if you're smarter than average, the government makes you wear an earphone that blasts piercing noises into your head to scramble your thoughts. If you're stronger or faster than average, you have to wear canvas sacks filled with birdshot to weigh you down. If you're prettier, you wear an ugly mask.

We're not quite there yet, but we've still got another seventy-five years. Those Sissy Swedes, Vikings-in-Volvos, are way ahead of us. They had a head start because they already all looked alike and had the same couple of names. Under their Euro-social-democracy, they've gone much further to ensure Swedish sameness and mash all Swedes into the middle, in every way. If a Swede gets industrious and starts making more money than the average Swede, a government Swede who looks just like him and has the same name withdraws the extra cash from his bank account and distributes it evenly among all the other Swedes who look just like him and have the same name. If a Swede builds a house bigger than average, the government appropriates half of it and moves in a Swedish family to share it equally. All the furniture and furnishings, of course, must be identical IKEA products.

We American Sissies are too numerous, divisive, and stoopitized to get as organized as Swedes, but that doesn't mean we love democratic mediocrity any less than they do. In disorganized default mode, we let the natural centripetal pull of democracy draw all things into the middle and the mainstream.

American Sissies don't really like eccentrics, individualists, geniuses, outlaws, freethinkers, and freewheelers. Sure, we celebrate these figures in our mythology, but that's because most of us aren't like that. When we meet actual eccentrics, individualists et al., they make us uncomfortable, or we go into how-dare-you-be-different, why-can't-you-look-and-act-and-think-like-everyone-else tongue clucking.

A Time Warner Cable ad of 2007 summed it up in one handy line: *"Share your individuality with people just like you."* There ya go.

We adore *The Sopranos* and gangsta rap videos, but if we met a real gangster or gangsta we'd be petrified. I know. As a journalist I had occasion to make several visits to the clubhouse of a certain outlaw gang whom I won't name because they're pretty touchy and I'm pretty Sissy. They called it a clubhouse, but I didn't see Spanky or Alfalfa or anyone vaguely resembling Buckwheat there. I saw guys who looked like fireplugs with tattoos, and guys who looked like human Dobermans and pit bulls, and guys who looked permanently very pissed with the world, and guys who looked permanently extraordinarily high. They looked like the guys who play violent gang members in movies and on TV, because they *were* the guys who play violent gang members in movies and on TV. No kidding, several of them were card-carrying members of the Screen Actors Guild. That's Funda-dome for ya.

The whole place vibrated with menace and the potential for mindless violence. It was like being inside a human hornets' nest. Like many gangs, these guys observed a code of ethics that was largely secret to outsiders. It seemed straightforward enough, though, since most of it apparently related to the ethics of how and when to beat people up. I was aware that it included a list of things I might do or say that could earn me an instant, savage beat-down. I didn't know what those things were, but that would make no difference. Ignorance is no defense before the outlaw. If I said the wrong thing, touched the wrong doorknob looking for the toilet, or just looked like somebody who ought to be beaten, the code of the outlaw would automatically kick in, and I'd get my face kicked. And it would not have been just one guy beating me. They all would have joined it. It's one of their codes. If one of them gets into a fight, they all get into it. It never happened, but the tattooed fireplug did once pin me to a wall and explain to me that, but for another member who was acting as my chaperone, I'd be dead. He did not explain why, and believe me I did not ask.

For all the talk Sissies have done over the past few decades about tolerating and in fact celebrating everyone's "differences," they clearly mean only those superficial differences of skin tone, language, dress, and so on that do not give anyone any *advantages* over everyone else. You rarely see Sissies celebrating such differences as inherited wealth and status, for example, or rare and flawless beauty, or yooge brains. Evidently there are good, correct differences and bad, incorrect differences. The good differences are the ones that don't really make a difference; they're just handy excuses for throwing a parade and taking a day off. The bad differences are the ones that actually make a difference.

Being Stoopits, we have to be reminded, once a year every year, to be proud of our tribal differences. Most tribes get a day to be proud, but gays, blacks, and women get a whole month. Does that mean you've got twenty-eight to thirty-one times more reasons to be proud than if you're just Puerto Rican or Irish? I mean it doesn't seem quite fair. If you're a gay black woman, you get three whole months a year to be proud of yourself. A het Italian guy gets only one day.

Can we talk a second about all these pride days and pride festivals and pride parades? Do you ever stop to ask yourself exactly what it is that you, in particular, you personally, have *done* to be so proud to be you on that day? You're proud because you're Irish, or gay, or female, or born in America? I mean, really, how much did you have to do with that? Isn't it a bit like being proud to breathe air? Isn't it somehow akin to the way our ultra-touchy young people are so concerned all the time about being "disrepected," yet don't do much of anything that might earn them any respect from anybody? Wouldn't it make more sense if you were out there marching because you're proud of what you've *done*, of your accomplishment and achievements? You personally, not you taking credit for what other members of your tribe did? The athletes parading around at the Olympics earned the right. They've done something to be proud of. You?

Anyway, for all this celebrating of differences, we don't really like or trust anyone who is *too* different, who stands out too much from the herd. We like people who seem a *little* more talented than average. Thus Madonna's otherwise inexplicable career, and LeRoy Neiman selling paintings before they're dry, and Russell Simmons getting to call the higgledy-piggledy doggerel on his TV show "poetry." We like our public intellectuals to be a *little* smarter than the rest of us—Malcolm Gladwell, Paul Krugman—but not freakishly brainy, unless it's offset by some humanizing debility, as with Stephen Hawking. If Hawking were as tall, strong, and handsome as he is smart, we'd hate his guts. When someone really special and freakishly gifted or blessed comes along, we like them only when there's some mitigating factor, a flaw, an Achilles' heel. We *admire* the Tiger Woods, the Luciano Pavarotti, the Princess Di, but we don't really *like* them until they choke in the clutch, reveal the steroid use, go through a messy divorce, land in rehab, die in a stoopit car accident, whatever.

Our current celebrity culture, obviously, represents the triumph of the mediocre and the middling. We worship celebrities, those individuals who are given special dispensation to stand out and be famous for...well, you tell me. Yet the whole industry of celebrity news and paparazzi exists solely to catch them in—or goad them into—the revelation that they're only people, as stoopit and weak as the rest of us. Sissies whose knowledge of the German language does not extend beyond "sauerkraut," "Heil Hitler," and "Siegfried and Roy" *absolutely* know what schadenfreude is. It is extremely important that celebrities reveal their flaws to us, because it validates the popular fantasy that if celebrities are just like us, we could be just like them.

As Christopher Lasch pointed out in *The Culture of Narcissism* (1978), this double-edged celebrity-worship/schadenfreude thing is textbook narcissistic behavior. Being narcissists, we identify with and fantasize associations with our glittering celebrities, but being *insecure* narcissists we also envy them and secretly kinda hate their guts and therefore rejoice in their flaws and failures. This is why the TV media gave us minute-by-minute, day-to-day updates on Martha Stewart's trial and incarceration over a period of months, and why photos of the celebuhilton bawling on her way to jail dominated the front pages of newspapers around the country, and why both TV and the tabloids simply could not stop killing Anna Nicole Smith over and over again for weeks and weeks after she managed to kill herself.

A big part of the genius of American-style democracy is that it's an attempt to balance the horizontal pull of the group and the vertical thrust of individuality, to encourage both group cohesion *and* individual fulfillment. The American Dream still attracts a constant flow of immigrants legal and illegal because this is one place—many people would say the only place in the world—where, with the right fuel mixture of ambition, talent, perseverance, and luck, the individual may achieve escape velocity. The gravitational pull of mediocrity is very strong, but it can be overcome.

Maybe it's because it's so hard to succeed at being an individual that so many successful individuals seem so hard. You don't *have* to be an A-dog egotistical blowhard to achieve—a Donald Trump, an Anna "Nuclear" Wintour, a Suge Knight—but it's one way to go.

Maybe that's just because we have so stoopitized the concept of personal fulfillment in this culture, vulgarizing it to equate with money, bling, and power. Success on these terms may not be personal fulfillment but it is clearly a license to be a dick.

Pop quiz. True or false:

- Three out of four American adults believe in Satan.
- Only two out of five believe in the evolution of humankind.
- Fewer than half understand that the earth orbits the sun.
- Half of them think that dinosaurs and humans walked the earth at the same time, just like in *The Flintstones.*
- Half of college-age Americans can't find the state of New York on a map, and even fewer can point to Afghanistan or Iraq.
- Only 23 percent of American college students can identify who James Madison was, but 98 percent know who Snoop Dogg is.
- More college students can name the Three Stooges than the three branches of the federal government.
- More Americans can identify Bart Simpson than Abraham Lincoln.
- The vocabulary of elementary through middle school kids has dropped to half what it was in 1945.
- In 2007, FOX began broadcasting the quiz show *Are You Smarter Than a 5th Grader?*
- George W. Bush, twice elected president, once said, "Rarely is the question asked: Is our children learning?"

Pencils down. Don't worry, Sissy, your answers will be graded on a steep curve to prevent any potential damage to your self-esteem.

Are Americans getting stoopiter every year? It sure is getting hard to think otherwise. But then, it sure is getting hard to think. Pretty soon FOX will be spinning off quiz shows like *Are You Smarter Than Linoleum?*

In 1835, Tocqueville remarked of America, "I do not believe that there is a country in the world where, in proportion to the population, there are so few uninstructed and at the same time so few learned individuals."

He wasn't exactly calling Americans Stoopits. He was commenting on the fact that a basic public education was available to almost everybody (though not free in his time), but almost nobody took it seriously because it had so little to do with work and getting ahead. Americans did not see the use of too much book-learning. They got some elementary schooling to pick up the three R's, enough to read the Bible and the newspaper and count their change at the feed store. Then they headed back out to the fields, or apprenticed themselves to some trade to learn practical, fungible knowledge.

The first public high schools were just being created in Tocqueville's day, but it would be quite a while before the average American extended his schooling past the elementary level. And only a minute elite had the time, resources, or inclination to be university trained and "learned" in the way Tocqueville meant—well read and well rounded, with a grounding in the arts and literature, history and philosophy, math and science. We forget now how very recently college was added to the average American's schooling. My siblings and I were the first generation in my family to go, in the 1960s and '70s.

A hundred seventy-five years after Tocqueville, the only real difference is that not only do we still have very few learned people among us, *we can hardly imagine what a truly learned person would be like, or why on earth you'd want to be one.* It's a role we don't much play in our fantasies. There's still not much point in being learned in America, and very little payoff for the scholar or intellectual. We still stress practical knowledge, even for post-graduates. Pointy-heads like me poke fun at schools like DeVry and the Refrigeration Institute, but the truth is that Harvard and Princeton and MIT are just as much vo-tech schools as they are.

Our most prestigious degrees are law and medicine, not coincidentally because they're keys to the most lucrative careers. A Ph.D. in dance or philosophy just sounds kind of ludicrous. The inevitable response is, "That's nice, but what are you gonna *do* with it?" Business majors outnumber English majors four to one. Our colleges and universities are geared to produce not learned folks but accountants, managers, and salespeople. Organization men and women.

Traditionally we've liked our sciences to be applied sciences, science we could use to build railroads, dig canals, bomb the stuffing out of the Japs, beat Ivan to the moon, speed up Internet porn. It was only quite recently, with the American empire up and humming, that we allowed our scientists to drift off into the la-la land of airy-fairy ideas like multidimensional string theory, and then only because it sounds so *Star Trek*, and if it gets us warp drive and lets us beam over to Baskin-Robbins and back we're cool with it. We'll even forgive the lack of Jetson flying cars if they give us home transporters. Beam me over, Colonel Sanders.

Going to art school means learning commercial art or computer graphics. We've never been high on high art. In the early years we just brought European culture here with us, and for a long time our wealthy, educated elite imported most anything really artsy-fartsy. Most Americans have never had much time for the arts. We had a nation and an empire to build, an indigenous population to shove out of our way, forests to clear, gold to pan, wells to drill, roads to pave, rivers to dam, animals to skin, cities to build, fortunes to make. And with our grounding in Puritanism and Calvinism, artsy-fartsiness was inherently suspect, probably sinful, and definitely frivolous anyway.

It was only in the twentieth century that America, and specifically New York City, became a major generator of the high arts and culture—a role it has now largely abandoned in the twenty-first century. For the most part, American culture has always been popular and commercial culture—pop music, popular dance crazes, Hollywood movies, TV, comic books, fashion, all that. It's one thing we really do have a genius for, even now, and one way we are the world's superpower. To this day, the big American newspapers call their arts sections "Arts & Leisure" or "Art & Entertainment" or such. Art all by itself, *ars gratia artsis fartsis*, remains something foreigners do.

We still learn just enough English to write ad copy and read those comic books. Anyone more fluent or literate than that is probably gay. Newt Gingrich, an "important" man, a man many people consider wise and scholarly, a man who has served as Speaker of the House and taught in university classrooms, a *Time* "Man of the Year," writes historical novels that are quite impossible to read or comprehend, they're so thick with grammatical errors and mangled syntax. His novel *Pearl Harbor*—co-written with a Ph.D. historian, please note—makes your brain ache with indecipherable doofisms like: "The boys had money in their pockets to burn and fresh in from the West Coast the obligatory photos with hula girls, sentimental silk pillows for moms and girlfriends, and ridiculous-printed shirts had sold like crazy." A leading political figure and/or a guy with a Ph.D. wrote that. And somebody with a career in publishing let it pass.

Knowledge for its own sake has always been highly suspect, possibly anti-American, and *definitely* gay. Americans just never saw the point of knowledge we can't use to make money. The well-rounded college grad who can hold his own in most any online discussion but can't apply what he knows to making a living is a loser. Even our philosophers have tended to have some sort of pragmatic, real-world application for their lofty thoughts—

politics (Tom Paine, Thomas Jefferson), law (Oliver Wendell Holmes), religion/spirituality/morality (a very crowded field), and all sorts of what we can call "self-help" philosophy (another crowded field, from Ben Franklin to John Dewey and William James to Felix Adler and Richard Rorty).

We don't like general knowledge. We want everyone to have a specialty, a focus, a precise area of expertise with a specific purpose. Over the past few decades, even the airy-fairy humanities are supposed to be if not exactly practical areas of study, at least "relevant," as in relevant to each student's own race, ethnicity, gender, sexuality, class, or other celebrated difference. The very term "humanities" is suspect, a white man's term, dripping with superiority and the imperialist lie that a white guy could possibly empathize with or understand other humans. As if, honky. And so the humanities have become segregated and specialized into womanities, homanities, blackmanities, asianities, and various other in-anities and in-humanities.

No manities, though. In a funny scene in the 2007 documentary *Indoctrinate U*, filmmaker Evan Coyne Maloney strolls into Women's Studies centers on various campuses and innocently asks for directions to the Men's Studies center. He's met with honest befuddlement, scornful laughter, or icy lesbionic hostility.

Granted, pretty much *all* education before, say, the 1970s was, in effect, Men's Studies. I was taught a top-down, Great White Man view of the world, not terribly different from what a Victorian student would have been taught. Modern America and ancient Greece were at the top of the stack of civilizations, followed by the British and Roman empires, then everybody else below. This view of the world drastically needed to be broadened and deepened, so that students could develop a more insightful, balanced, and nuanced understanding of the world's rich panoply of cultures, classes et al., turning the world around and around in their minds like a Rubik's Cube, seeing it from all angles.

Yeah, that would be great.

In reality, American college professors are no less Anvil Heads than the rest of us. Balanced and nuanced are not in their vocabulary. They're as dogmatic and groupthinking as any Sissies in America, and the view of the world they impart to their students is as pinched, narrow, and proudly closed-minded as any other fundamentalist belief system.

College students may not learn where Afghanistan and Iraq are, but they sure do learn—and learn not to question openly— Professor Sister Right-on's Marxist-Lesbianist *political opinions* about Afghanistan and Iraq, and everything else. Half of the young Americans who enter college drop out before getting a degree. This figure upsets a lot of people, but maybe it's just as well. Because it is without question that *American campuses have become giant Petri dishes where many aspects of our Sissy culture are cultured.* A kid who drops out halfway to a degree might end up only half-a-Sissy.

We all know how this happened. Back in my day, the 1960s into the '70s, campuses were centers of youth rebellion—the New Left, the free speech movement, the antiwar protests. For a while there, the Revolution—actual armed-uprising, fighting-in-the-streets, hang-the-landlord-from-the-lamppost rebellion— seemed imminent and inevitable.

But some funny things happened on the way to the Revolution. The students and downtrodden proletariat failed to connect the way the students had envisioned. Large fissures also opened up between the white revolutionaries and the black ones. The tiny minority of white revolutionaries who actually resorted to violence scared the hell out of everyone else, for whom the Revolution had always been more theory and attitude than action. Call it bullshevism. Hippie utopias from the Haight to the East Village crumbled in the face of harsh urban reality. Pot and acid gave way to heroin and cocaine. Woodstock turned almost overnight into Altamont.

Most important, when the draft ended and the Vietnam War sputtered toward its shambolic end, a huge motivation for rebellion disappeared, too. No longer facing death halfway around the world, an awful lot of rebellious youth realized they had nothing much else to rebel about. Most cut their hair and joined the straights at the office. Jerry Rubin negotiated the transformation from Yippie to yuppie with marvelous ease, and Black Panther Bobby Seale went from preaching armed revolt to shilling for his own brand of Bobbyque sauce.

Others stayed on campus, transitioning from students to faculty, and continued to pursue their largely theoretical and rhetorical revolution, which came to be known in polite circles as a "cultural revolution." Some good things came out of or were encouraged by the cultural revolution at first, including the women's movement, the gay rights movement, and a generally heightened awareness of the rich diversity of ethnicities and cultures in the world.

Then, inevitably, it all got stoopitized and Sissified. The free speech movement was turned inside out and became politically correct "speech code" censorship. Equal rights was Sissified into victimology and identity politics. Diversity was dumbed down into divisiveness. All of it bubbling in a thick stew of sullen, knee-jerk, head-bobbing, campus-Marxist I-hate-my-daddy anti-Americanism.

That sort of attitude is more or less expected when you're twenty. It's kind of embarrassing when you're forty or fifty. Whatever else you might think of that professor Ward Churchill, the one who caused so much uproar calling the dead of 9/11 "little Eichmanns" and getting his picture took cradling an automatic weapon and claiming to be an American Indian, you cannot deny he was a putz who got permanently stuck in the '60s.

No doubt that's why these folks never leave the campus. They have spent the past thirty-odd years preaching their bullshevism in the classroom—not just in history or political science courses but in physics and biology and chemistry and horticulture and all across the curriculum. And over the years they've been joined by the next generation of professors whom they sissified and stoopitized when they were students, further consolidating the fundamentalist groupthink on many, if not most, American campuses.

In my day there was a de facto system of checks and balances on campus. We students were the antiestablishment, anti-American protesters, and the administration and faculty played the role of the hated establishment adults. Now they're *all* antiestablishment and anti-American. The only "rebellious youth" on campus nowadays are the Young Republicans, the Ayn Rand book club, and the Christians.

To ensure the divisiveness and lack of mutual understanding now called diversity, students on many campuses are actually segregated by victim group, living in segregated dorms, effectively pursuing segregated curricula, socializing at segregated events, and at many campuses even celebrating with segregated graduation ceremonies. You could rename a bunch of these institutions Jim Crow University. How this prepares kids for life in multiculti twenty-first-century America is anyone's guess. They'd be better prepared to live in the Deep South in the 1880s.

The one type of diversity not celebrated is a diversity of opinion.

In the early years of the Bolshevik revolution, Lenin declared any opinion he didn't like "bourgeois," which gave him license to silence it. Hugo Chávez, Venezuela's fauxialist cartoon caudillo, later appropriated the same term in shutting down any TV stations or newspapers that criticized him.

Debate is stifled in pretty much the same way on campuses today. The Bolsheviks are gone, but the bullsheviks rule the campus with iron fists. Students who question a professor's political dogma are openly ridiculed in class, instructed to seek psychological counseling, and threatened with various kinds of censure, and they live with the fear that their grades may suffer simply because they questioned comrade professor. Student publications that question or defy the bullsheviks are denounced, defunded, disciplined, and sometimes destroyed.

Meanwhile, the students are no slouches either when it comes to censoring ideas and opinions they don't want to hear. They'll shout down any speaker challenging their cherished beliefs. They wield ugly terms like "racist" and "fascist" and "homophobic" with shocking abandon to end debate and defame anyone who disagrees with them.

And the school administration backs them up with campus speech codes that flagrantly violate the First Amendment. Syracuse University banned "sexually suggestive staring" and "sexual, sexist, or heterosexist remarks or jokes." Brown University outlawed speech that might cause "feelings of impotence, anger, or disenfranchisement," even if unintentional. Colby College prohibited any expression that might cause a student to feel a loss of self-esteem. The University of North Dakota defined anything that caused "psychological discomfort, embarrassment, or ridicule" as harassment. Censorship got so bad that many schools set up designated "free speech zones," isolated areas usually on the back-ass fringe of the campus where students could actually voice their opinions and speak their minds. Woo hoo.

Last time I checked, there was nothing in the Constitution or the Bill of Rights guaranteeing Americans freedom from *discomfort, embarrassment, or hurt feelings*. But then, the Constitution and Bill of Rights were written by imperialist, capitalist, slave-owning, hate-mongering white men.

Since our schools reject those documents, I propose a new code.

The Sissy Bill of Rights

- You have the right to agree with everything we tell you.
- You have the right to think what we tell you to think.
- You have the right not to learn, hear, or think anything you don't already agree with.
- You have the right to find any thought, word, gesture, action, or look offensive.
- You have the right to be protected from discomfort, anger, embarrassment, hurt feelings, differences of opinion, challenges to your preconceptions, and anything else that might somehow cause a lessening of your self-esteem.
- You have the right to censor any of the aforementioned thoughts, words, gestures, actions, or looks.

This isn't higher education, it's higher day-care center. Let's admit it and move on.

Remember that older guy who banged on the bar and insisted on his right to hear only opinions he already agreed with? Had to be a retired professor. The younger guy with the more open mind was probably a dropout.

It's true that Bible colleges and places like Brigham Young University exert the same fascistoid control over their students' brains and bodies, but at least they're not hypocrites about it. They're proud to be fundamentalist indoctrination centers. Kids going into Bob Jones University know exactly what they're gonna get, and that's what they want.

Still, if the political poles flipped on all the other campuses and they became bastions of monolithic conservatism, would the knee-jerk and censorship be just as bad? You know it. It's the Way of the Sissy. Give any like-minded group its own little fiefdom, with unlimited power to control the minds and bodies of a captured audience, and the self-righteous, censorious hive mind kicks into top gear. It's not just the stoopit regions of our brains that vibrate in synch when we join groups.

In fact, after 9/11 the poles did shift a little. Professors Ward Churchill and Sister Right-on, trapped in amber since the '60s, cocooned in their campus-lefty bubble, failed to notice that many American Sissies—including a number of their students—had gone all patriotic and Cold War paranoid again. The professors kept banging out their usual anti-American I-hate-my-daddy cant, embracing the cause of the downtrodden terrorist and scolding American Sissies for bringing 9/11 on themselves.

Post–9/11, that wasn't going down as smoothly as it once had. The conservatives jumped at the chance to do a little censoring of their own. Some professors who made critical noises about the War on Terror found themselves accused of sedition and treason. Their jobs and even their lives were threatened. College administrators, accurately reading the moods of the politicians and alumni on whom their jobs depended, raced to the lectern to denounce their teachers as unpatriotic. Student groups who protested the war found themselves under scrutiny for possible violations of Homeland Security rules.

For a while there, with the war fever and hysteria on high boil, the shoe had turned and the worm was on the other foot. It was a very handy demonstration that under the superficial veneer of a "polarized" red state–blue state Sissy Nation, *knee-jerk is knee-jerk, and free speech is free only when it's speech the Sissy agrees with.*

Young people are notoriously self-righteous. They think they know everything. That's why your college years are supposed to be a time of intellectual exploration and growth. Students are supposed to be engaged by new knowledge and challenged by ideas and opinions they haven't already formed. Forced to think through their knee-jerk cant and articulate their views in something a little more sophisticated than bumper-sticker slogans.

Nowadays a great many go only to have their preconceptions confirmed and their indoctrination into knee-jerk, head-bobbing groupthink completed, whether the groupthink is of the Bible-thumping or the flag-burning persuasion.

Some of us miss the old model of the campus as the one place in your life where intellectual curiosity is encouraged, but maybe we're also missing the point. Colleges that coddle, infantilize, encourage the victim whining and close the minds of their students are simply preparing them for life as adult American Sissies. If they were encouraged to think, to challenge themselves and Professor Sister Right-on, to question, to debate, to articulate their views, they'd come out misanthropic misfits here inside Fundadome, making themselves miserable and everyone else uncomfortable.

Back when only a tiny, elite minority of young Americans went to college, none of this would have much mattered. Before World War II, a mere 5 percent of high school graduates went on to college. Colleges were like sphincters that admitted only the best and brightest. Well, theoretically. Idiot sons of the rich and powerful could always find a spot at Harvard, Princeton, or Yale. Like George W. Bush, Yale Man. If I were a Yalie, I'd be right pissed about that. Anyway, when this tiny elite graduated, they were expected to run the country and the corporations, while all the rest of us milked the cows, pushed the pencils, filled the tank, and popped out the cannon fodder.

After World War II, in an ongoing program to ensure that the maximum percentage of people living inside Fundadome had completed their indoctrination as Stoopit Sissies, colleges and universities were thrown open to pretty much anyone who applied. They went from being sphincters to giant Hoovers. Around 75 percent of high school graduates now go on to college.

This has required some tinkering at the lower levels of the education system. For one thing, graduating from high school was made easier. Courses were dumbed down, grades curved. Nowadays you can pretty much graduate from many a public high school by showing up a required minimum of days and not getting caught assaulting anyone while you're there. Or at least not convicted. Okay, maybe once, but not twice. Unless you apologize and submit to professional counseling.

Obviously, we had to make getting into college easier, too. So the all-important SAT had to be "recentered," a polite euphemism for stoopitized. They also dropped "Aptitude" and "Achievement" from SAT lingo, because the words wounded the self-esteem of students who were aptitude- or achievement-challenged. SAT now stands for Sissy Acceptance Treat.

The SAT was used as early as the 1930s to help sift out those applicants who were "college material" from those who'd just end up failing out of college anyway, so why encourage them to go in the first place. It is impossible now to imagine our Sissy culture passing such an ego-crushing judgment on its young people. That half of them never *complete* college, and many of those are stuck with cruel student loan payments and no high-paying job to help them meet those commitments, is beside the point. In an egalitarian culture, we want every kid to *think* he can get a college degree, even if half of them won't, because it's important for their self-esteem to know that college isn't just for some kids, it's for all kids...even though it's evidently only for half of them. But never mind. What's important is the *perception* that all kids are equal, that no kid is better "college material" than any other kid.

Lookit, our public education system was basically always meant to operate as a network of warehouses and holding pens for American youth. Classrooms are waiting rooms where they dawdle until they can get out, get a job, get knocked up, get arrested, get killed in action, whatever. It's never been a mystery why kids get bored, restless, hyper, and aggro there. In my day they'd rap you on the knuckles, or send you to detention or reform school. Now we diagnose you as ADD/ADHD and write you a scrip.

School isn't the be-all and end-all of a person's education. Students teach themselves. The best schools and teachers inspire, encourage, and facilitate the student's desire to learn about the world. The great preponderance of bad and mediocre schools kill that desire and make learning seem boring and useless.

The whole point of the human brain having developed extra wrinkles and higher functions was to create an intellect freed from all the animal business of instinct and regulating the body's functions—the second-by-second necessities of survival that use up most of the brains of most of the brained organisms on the planet. The human brain is supposed to be free to dream, theorize, wonder, question, analyze, criticize.

It is that very freedom, and those very functions, that Sissies mistrust about the intellect. The fundamentalists within Christianity and Islam literally demonize the intellect. Being too smart and critical is a sign that Satan's gotten hold of you and lured you into the sin of "intellectual pride." But there are all sorts of secular fundamentalists, all over the political and social spectrum, whose opinions are just as faith-based, and who are just as resistant to intellectual debate. If you question or think too hard about their pro-life fundamentalism, their Green fundamentalism, their pro- or antiwar fundamentalism, you're Satan's helpmeet.

In a real sense they're right. The curious intellect *is* the enemy of blind faith. As a young Catholic, the more I thought about all the tenets of the religion I was supposed to accept on faith, the less Catholic I became. Numerous religious philosophers through the ages have tried heroically to explain how the free intellect can happily coexist with blind faith, and they always fall short. All arguments *for* faith end up being proclamations *of* faith. They can't help but be so. That's what faith is. It's not thought, it's belief. Even books like *The Secret*, with all their palaver about "thinking" your way to happiness and riches, use the words "thoughts" and "thinking" interchangeably with "belief" and "faith."

So it should be obvious: *The more fundamentalist and "faith-based" we have become in all aspects of our society, the stoopiter.*

Optimists try to counter all this and buck us up about our apparent dumbing-down. We're not getting stoopiter, they claim, it's the nature of knowledge, intelligence, and learning that's changing. As a civilization we're evolving past the need for verbal or math skills, because we're becoming post-literate, visual, digital, kinetic. We don't need to add or spell because we have computers to do that for us now. We don't need to hold useless trivia like geography or the workings of the solar system in our heads anymore because we've got the Internet at our fingertips, remembering all that stuff for us. We're free to apply our brains to other pursuits...like, you know, eBay and rap lyrics.

TV and computer games are making us smarter, optimists claim, not dumber. It's just a different kind of smarts. The three R's trained our brains to think linearly, tracking one thought at a time from the start of a sentence to the end, from one side of the equals sign to the other. Our brains learned to see everything in straight lines—history, progress, our own lives, time itself. TV shows like *The Sopranos* and *24* train our brains to multitask, to follow numerous squiggly lines simultaneously, to form nests of associations and connections that make sense out of apparent confusion and chaos. Computer games train us to think more kinetically, speeding up and sharpening our hand-eye-brain coordination. All of which adapts us better for life in the fast-track, chaotic twenty-first century.

That'd all be nice if it were true. But empirical data and anecdotal observation suggest otherwise. In the pre-Sissy era most of us were "unlearned," and plenty of us were, in fact, stupid. That's humanity. But it's only in the Sissy Age that we've had the will and the means to *actively and programmatically stoopitize and Sissify ourselves* in such vast numbers. Now we can't read, write, add, subtract, *or* think in a straight line—*and* we're so stoopitized we don't know how stoopit we are—*and* we're touchy about it if anyone brings it up. The Stoopit Sissy hat trick.

When *The Flintstones* originally aired back when I was a kid, everyone knew it was a silly cartoon. Now half of us believe it was paleolithic reality TV. TV and games seem only to be adapting us to watch more TV and play more games. Why would they do otherwise? It'd be bad for business.

Here inside Fundadome, maybe being really good at watching TV and playing games are key survival skills. How well they prepare us to deal with the rest of the world, the world Beyond Fundadome, is a good question. We better hurry up and expand Fundadome soon, so that the whole world is World World.

What I'm calling the Age of the Sissy incorporates the widely known concept of the postmodern era. "Postmodern" has a fittingly apocalyptic ring, like "postnuclear." There's something appropriately deflated and anticlimactic about an age that isn't described for what it is in itself but for the age it comes "post."

Yet another polite euphemism, postmodernism stands for:

"We've run out of new ideas. We lost our faith in progress. We pushed civilization as far as it could go, and it blew up in our faces. We're just going to stop here and rest awhile, not try anything new or adventurous, maybe just fiddle around with rearranging old ideas."

Like Sissitude, this notion that we were entering a postmodern era emerged in the years after World War II, with the first inklings that the modern age had reached its apex and blown itself all to hell in that cataclysmic affair. Over the next couple of decades the notion spread that many of the ideas and products of modern progress had had deleterious to disastrous consequences, requiring a pause for a general rethink.

After all, the modern social engineering projects called Communism and National Socialism had massacred tens of millions and brought misery and enslavement to tens of millions more. Modern technological progress had produced war machinery of unspeakable power that now threatened us with Mutual Assured Destruction. Meanwhile, modern industry, agriculture, and the population explosion, which was made possible by modern advances in health and nutrition, were killing the planet more gradually.

Modern architecture had seeded our cities with cold, anonymous monoliths of glass and steel. The modern city was a forbidding urban jungle, the modern suburb a zombie wasteland.

Modern arts had pushed experimentation to the point where painting was obsolete, music was noise you couldn't hum or whistle anymore, and literature was an indecipherable babble.

Even God was dead, killed by modern science and secularism.

In his book *Art & Discontent* (1991), art historian Thomas McEvilley made a good case that "modern" and "postmodern" are just contemporary terms for oscillations Western Civ has been going through at least since the Greeks of the sixth century BC. Cultures have their modern periods when they're being aggressive, progressive, optimistic, creative, and innovative. History is seen as moving humanity toward perfection, and geniuses and artists are honored as models and examples of what we can all be. Then the envelope gets pushed as far as it'll go, the momentum is lost, and the culture settles into a postmodern pause that's more passive, skeptical of progress and perfectibility and genius, less sure of itself or its purpose, more backward-looking. At some point, after this nap period, culture gets a shot in the arm and a kick in the pants and gets busy and innovative and modern again. And the cycle repeats.

More recently, some people have been saying we're entering a "post-postmodern" phase, which as near as I can tell means they're sick of both modernism and postmodernism. Let us not speak of it again until they can come up with a better name for it.

The modern era had its downsides, no question. It's hard to see, however, how postmodernism is a great improvement.

Modern art, for example, was all about creation and exploration. Postmodern art is all copying and quotation. Modern art gave us Picasso, Matisse, Monet, Gauguin, Renoir, Ernst, Klimt,

Grosz, Dalí, Dix, Magritte, Kandinsky, de Kooning, Chagall, De Chirico, Klee, Modigliani, Rothko, Hopper, Johns, Frankenthaler, Rauschenberg, Lichtenstein, Bacon, Dubuffet, Stella, Pollock, Warhol, and a bunch of others.

Postmodern art gave us…Jenny Holzer's bumper-sticker sloganeering, Julian Schnabel's intentionally ugly paintings, Jeff Koons's topiary puppies, and Damien Hirst's dissected sharks. All housed in postmodern art museums that look like the architect ripped up a bunch of pages from an illustrated atlas of architecture through the ages, piled the scraps on his desk, and said, "My work here is done. You know where to mail the check."

It would be stoopit and just plain incorrect to argue that modern art was "good" and postmodern "bad" (although that's what Schnabel proudly called his paintings). Still, a lot of postmodern art is undeniably Sissy art, art made with a big sigh and a little shrug, an expression of cultural exhaustion, self-doubt, and fatalism handily summed up by the artist Allison Hetter, who gave the movement its motto, "Everything's been done already." In postmodern politics, the equivalent was Francis Fukuyama's idea that we'd reached "the end of history."

Now take God. The modern age didn't really kill God. It just challenged his fans to a debate they couldn't win. In the postmodern age, they don't even try to debate. When it comes to God, postmodern is just another way of saying premodern, the return of a medieval age of faith.

It's true that the modern age's boundless optimism in its ingenious technocrats—the experts who would solve all our problems, cure all our ills, create a perfect world and fill it with perfected human beings—seemed to end up at a profound disrespect for both the world and human beings. The Nazis thought they were experts on what the perfect human being was and how to build one, and look where that got us. The Commies were convinced they knew how to build the perfect society.

Modern architects and designers built their buildings and designed their model cities and even their chairs as projects in social engineering. They knew what was good for us, whether we liked it or not.

You: "I hate this ugly, depressing apartment complex."

The architect: "Shut up. I designed it for maximum density as well as optimum pedestrian traffic flow at peak hours. Living here will make you a more efficient human being."

You: "Ow. This chair is ugly, it hurts my back, and if I sit on it for more than five minutes my butt develops bedsores."

The designer: "Shut up. You're not sitting in it right. This chair improves your circulation and breathing. Plus I won a very important international design award for it. You saying your butt knows more about chairs than an international panel of experts?"

After the nuclear power plant at Three Mile Island melted down in 1979, scaring the hell out of us not far away in Baltimore, I had a long talk with a nuclear physicist who was outraged that because of a single mistake we foolish laypeople were expressing doubts about nuclear power. Nuclear power was good for us! Nuclear power was the future! Nuclear power was safe and clean! We didn't know what we were talking about! We should just shut up and let the experts create a better world for us!

Too bad I didn't know him anymore when Chernobyl happened. I would have loved to hear what he'd have said about that.

So if the megalomaniacal fuck-ups of egotistical technorati in the twentieth century taught us anything, it was that we needed to better educate ourselves about these things, ask smarter questions, not accept their jargon and pronouncements on faith alone. That's the postmodern spirit, right?

Sigh.

Instead, we called a general retreat—from progress, from thinking, from the world. We erected Fundadome over the land

and the culture our empire-building ancestors left us and settled down to our trivial pursuits and petty squabbles.

We don't much strive for greatness or think big thoughts anymore. We don't trust the impulse. The great scientific and technological advances of the Sissy Age have been the Segway, the cell phone, the iPod, the laptop, the BlackBerry, the Xbox, Viagra, leaf blowers, hi-def plasma TV screens wide enough for a dozen starving Somalians to sleep on, cloned pets, and genetically modified tomatoes that grow, slice, and eat themselves in your kitchen, then clean up afterward.

This is not some Luddite argument that any one of these devices is bad. Although a few, like the Segway and the leaf blower and the self-growing tomato, surely qualify as what the inventor Kenji Kawakami calls "unuseless"—tools that work, but you have to ask what they say about you that you'd want to own and use them.

No, the point is *the culture we create* when we plug ourselves in constantly, surround ourselves with and obsess about these things. The way we use these devices to isolate and insulate ourselves—to escape permanently from reality into virtual reality. To escape from other human beings.

Playtime, downtime, personal time, fantasy, and games are all necessary to our mental and physical well-being. But they're supposed to be respites from our daily routines, not *be* our daily routines.

Take the iPod. Nice invention. I got me a Nano for use at the gym, because the music at the gym is so loud and so bad it was keeping me out of the gym. At my age, a guy has to work at staying fit, and if I was going to do that I had to block out the gym's noise. The gym is the only place I use it, though.

More and more Sissies use their iPods to block out the entire world from the moment they step out the door to when they get back home. I know, I know—it's a loud, crowded world. Why not bring your music along if you can?

Because walking around the world with your earbuds constantly in is a supremely antisocial act that's come to look quite casual and normal because it's ubiquitous. Blocking out all the auditory signals of the world around you is a form of voluntary autism. A way of turning reality into silent images, like a big TV with the sound off. It's not reality, just reality TV with no sound. In your little, passive way you're dehumanizing the people all around you, and dehumanizing yourself. They're not really people. They're just figures moving around on your reality TV screen. You're not really there, either.

Also, as Vonnegut pointed out forty-odd years ago, having music constantly blasting inside your cranium is not doing much good for your ability to think. But of course not-thinking is the Sissy way.

Lots of people use their cell phones as a way to carry their own personal fundadome around with them, clearing a quasi-privacy bubble for themselves. We use cells the way we use our excess flesh, *as a passive-aggressive demand for extra space and extra attention.*

It's amazing how people yammering into their cells in public can block out everyone and everything around them. Blabbering loudly on your cell also reduces everyone around you to not just eavesdropper but audience, complicit in helping you construct your inane, faux-celebrity fantasy life. Who's that person on her cell? Is it someone important? Hey, it's *me*! You wanna take your picture with me on my cell-cam?

The less we have in the way of identifiably individual and personal lives, the more we've made those lives public. Shouting into your cell in a room full of strangers is just one of many forms of public confession. Like we're all trying to convince ourselves that we're real individuals, with real emotional crises and real love lives and real passions. Our poetry, and a great deal of our fiction, is confessional now. It's not poetry or literature, it's a public diary. Poetry readings are indistinguishable from a bunch of people on their cells. We go on *Oprah* and call-in radio and any other forum offered to confess our inane secrets and bland sins.

Like the iPod and the cell phone, the laptop is a great invention. It's how we use it that's disturbing. People now carry their laptops everywhere with them because they get wicked withdrawal symptoms from being unconnected to their e-mail and MySpace friendsters for more than fifteen minutes. This is of course why the entirety of Fundadome now provides wireless access. WiFi is the new methadone, supplied to all the cyberjunkies to keep them from going into reality seizures.

The coffeehouse was invented in the Islamic world in the sixteenth century and quickly spread through Europe. It was a social gathering place, where people met to chat over a cuppa joe. Now when you walk into a Starbucks or any Starbucks knockoff, people are still gathered there, but it's as silent as the crypt. Because they're all on their laptops, with their earbuds in. All gathered in the same room, but each sealed in his/her own personal bubble, oblivious of the others and the surroundings. Their collecting there is a vestigial activity, an atavistic echo of our more social primate past, a gathering of ghosts in the machine, zombies at the mall.

I suppose it's good they get out of the house at all. I'm a writer. I work at home. Pretty much seven days a week, every week, I'm in a corner of my kitchen, leaning into my computer, tap-tap-tapping, sending and receiving e-mails, browsing the Net. And I swear there are days when I dread going out the door for a meeting, or even just to buy groceries. The Internet has given me a mild case of agoraphobia. I jump out of my skin when the phone rings.

But why should I go out at all? Everyone I know or do business with is plugged in. I could get along entirely without walking out my front door. Do my work, have my playtime, interact with my friends, do my banking, pay my bills, order in food and clothing and toiletries, all without leaving the kitchen.

And increasingly we do. When we're out among people, we don't really have any contact with them. When we go out the door, the world has been replaced by its simulacrum, no more real than SimCity. Our friends are all friendsters, our "community" the community of fellow MySpace users.

A friend of mine let me eavesdrop for a couple months on her MySpace account. I know I'm an old fart, kids, but your definition of a community has to be a lot looser than mine to call MySpace a community, or 99.9 percent of the "people" you "meet" there "friends." A community is a social network of some sort, people who've come together because they live in the same place, or because they share interests or needs. It's a concept that was already stretched pretty thin—the heavy metal community, the crossword fanatics community—but when you get to the point where you're speaking seriously about the MySpace community or the Facebook community, you've pretty clearly lost all sense of what a social network is.

This is not to say that online communities don't exist—they surely do. They're formed by people who really do have some common interest, affinity, or need, who use the Internet to network and communicate and share knowledge relevant to their group. The Internet is just a tool for them, an updated version of the telephone or newsletter. Their community doesn't exist *because of* and *solely on* the Internet.

MySpace is a bulletin board for bands, DJs, rappers, and sex workers trolling for clients. Good on them. Among the "friends" my friend attracted, the ratio of (probably) actual human beings to those kinds of commercial enterprises looked to be about one to every hundred. And half the probable humans were geeky cyberstalkers using some of the oldest trawling lines in the history of mankind—"I'm an art photographer and I think you've got great bone structure and..."

I'm pretty sure that the more time you spend putzing around

on MySpace and Facebook pretending to be part of that community, the less interest you'll have in getting involved with a community of fellow human beings. Especially if every time you go out the door you've got your earphones in and your laptop in your man-purse.

In his 1909 story "The Machine Stops," the British novelist E. M. Forster, not generally known as a sci-fi writer—he wrote books like *Howards End* and *A Passage to India*—looked a hundred years into the future and got a pretty good glimpse of what we've become. He predicted a future in which humans, soft and hairless, are cocooned in solitary underground cells they rarely leave, each perfectly safe and comfortable and climate-controlled, all hooked up to a giant computer that provides everything they desire—music, food, light—at the touch of a button. They communicate through what are in effect e-mail and iChat, and have become so comfortable in their isolation, so used to experiencing everything through the Machine, that they have "terrors of direct experience." They flinch in disgust from the rare touch of another human.

The digitalization of life here inside Fundadome was preceded by what in some ways has been an even more radical flight from the real: *the disneyfication of our physical surroundings, the actual real estate, into safe, manicured unreal estate.*

The mallification and suburbanization of America were the start. They're ancient history now, so let's just note how integral and critical they were to the more general process of Sissification. The explosion of mall-fed suburbs began, naturally, after World War II. American cities had been slowly excreting suburbs for a century by then, but this was the big bang of suburbs, built farther and farther away from the cities, more and more independent from them. It was driven by the population bubble of the baby boom, and made possible by postwar government home loans, new quick-and-easy construction methods, the creation of the interstate highway network, and the rapid proliferation of new manufacturing areas and anonymous office parks and chain stores and restaurants and so on.

Almost overnight, millions of Americans were living in an entirely new physical and social environment, a new plane of bland unreality different from anything that had come before—the farm, the small town, or the big city. With their identical street plans and identical houses and identical office parks and identical shops in identical malls, the suburbs provided the perfect environment to reinforce corporate consumerist conformism. Many new so-called planned communities regulated this conformism down to the type of grass or shrub you could grow, and the color of the fake shutters on your "choice" of Type A, B, or C ranch house.

It took no time for the downsides of suburbia—boredom, alienation, a general dulling of both personal and social life, all that—to become so well known as to pass into cliché. It took a little longer to realize that the suburbanization and Sissification of America were also reducing many of America's small towns, the once proud icons of American life, to quaintly vestigial social organs—almost literally Potemkin villages—and simultaneously sucking the life out of America's cities, especially the older, industrialized ones.

The effect on the big cities was important because, much as the millions of Americans who didn't live in them didn't like to admit it, the big cities were America's nerve centers, its hubs of industry, commerce, communications, culture—and, in their mix of cultures and classes and ethnicities, workshops for democracy itself. By the 1970s, many of the factories, businesses, workers, and managers had dispersed to new suburbs, and to office and industrial parks around the country (when their jobs were not banished to outside Fundadome altogether).

The cities' economies collapsed. Their very reason to exist

was questioned. Big cities were now seen as drags on the economy, nothing but crime- and drug-ridden ghettoes for the urban poor.

New York City, the most densely urban of American urban spaces, is a classic example. Economically, it hit its twentieth-century peak by 1960. It's strange now to think of the city as a major manufacturing center, but in the mid-twentieth century there were a million light-manufacturing jobs in the city—compared with around a hundred thousand now. The port was still busy, lower Manhattan was a world financial hub, and Midtown bristled with shoulder-to-shoulder corporate headquarters. The music industry, movies, TV and radio, advertising, Broadway, the fashion and garment industries, the thriving bohemias below Fourteenth Street all added to the city's unrivaled reputation as the glittering, bustling "capital of the world."

The bottom fell out by the 1970s. The abandonment began as a trickle in the late '60s and accelerated into a flood over the next two decades. The city lost two-thirds of its Fortune 500 corporate headquarters, its docks were rotting husks, its light industrial zones were abandoned wastelands. Its dominance in other sectors once identified solely with Manhattan—advertising and marketing, entertainment, publishing, even finance—eroded. The middle class and professionals followed the jobs, leaving the city to the poor, the "ethnic," the artists and punks. For most of the thirty years leading up to 9/11, New York City's unemployment rate was consistently higher than the national average. There were actually more jobs in the city in 1969 than in 2000.

The city lapsed into bankruptcy in the 1970s, and President Gerald Ford famously refused to bail it out. Basic services, from garbage pickup to filling potholes to public transportation, were barely maintained. The police, courts, and schools appeared to be overrun and scarcely able to function. Whole areas of the South Bronx, central Brooklyn, and the Lower East Side looked like bombed-out war zones. It's no coincidence that the film *Escape from New York* appeared in 1981. Although set in the future (1997) and not principally shot in New York, but on the equally ravaged streets of St. Louis, its vision of a burned-out Manhattan as a big loony bin run by criminals wasn't so very far from reality.

Meanwhile, many other American cities were collapsing in the same basic way—Los Angeles, St. Louis, Detroit, Pittsburgh, Baltimore, D.C. et al.

Clearly, if they were going to survive, these cities needed to reinvent and repurpose themselves. They needed to do whatever they could to lure those Sissies back in from the suburbs.

And they did. They Sissified themselves. They transformed themselves from dark, frightening sin pits to clean, safe, generic, sub/urban theme parks. And the Sissies have indeed come flooding back in.

In a stroke of genius, New York City chose Disney itself to spearhead its makeover in the mid-1990s. No lesser outfit had the mojo for such an immense task. Six Flags, Busch Gardens? No, it had to be Disney. And it had to begin on Manhattan's most notoriously declined area, Forty-second Street, which over the previous thirty years had sunk into a zone of raw sin and depravity. Disney touched the street with its magic wand and in a shower of fairy dust those thirty years of scuzz and scum vanished. A new Forty-second Street emerged, clean and safe and brightly lit, a family fun center that's very much what a re-creation of Forty-second Street would look like inside Disneyland itself.

From that most symbolic beachhead, the themeparking of the city unfolded. A glittering new city, bright and safe and clean, was laid out over the grid of the old one. Decades of grime and grit were whisked away. Entire blocks of dark old buildings were razed, and shiny new towers reared up out of the deep construction pits. Miles of rotting waterfront became leafy parks. Streets that had felt unsafe at any hour were now well-lit boulevards inviting midnight strolls.

Sissies now competed to pay astronomical prices to fill new luxury condominiums as quickly as they could be built. The Manhattan that had previously daunted visitors with its global riot of colors, tastes, and smells now offered the soothing familiarity of Starbucks and Olive Gardens, Kmarts and Pottery Barns. The Manhattan that had always felt foreign to the rest of America, a wild frontier town on the edge of civilization, rapidly tamed itself, learned manners, snuggled a little closer to Sissy Nation every day.

It all happened so fast that to locals it looked like one of those time-lapse nature films where flowers and plants shoot up out of the forest floor and burst open in a cloud of pretty colors. Even the trauma of 9/11, rather than retard the pace of change, only spurred the city on.

At the start of his second term as mayor in January 2006, Michael Bloomberg proudly noted the remarkable resurgence New York City had achieved since 9/11. Tourism had bounced back to historic highs, unemployment was declining for the first time in decades, and the housing market was riding an astounding boom. New York City, once referred to as "New Calcutta," was looking more like New Club Med.

Sociologists Richard Lloyd and Terry Nichols Clark call this new species of Sissified urbanity the "city as an entertainment machine." Amenities-rich simulacra of their former selves, they are Potemkin cities that use local color—Baltimore's historic waterfront, Detroit's Motown and Motor City legacies—as quaint design elements. Los Angeles turned to Universal Studios for Citywalk, a miniaturized, mallized replica of...Los Angeles. An idealized La-La Land where people do in fact walk, unlike in the real L.A., and without the bums, gangs, and so on that made the real L.A. feel unsafe and unpleasant even when you saw it only from the inside of your SUV. Once bustling hubs of riotous, chaotic activity, more and more American cities are going this way, becoming Disney or Universal cities.

Yeah, they probably had to Sissify to survive. But they've lost more than their grit and grime. They've lost their character and their souls. What made them unique is glimpsed now only in their nostalgically themed bars and tourist attractions. Everything else—the streets, the buildings, the shops—is generic. Every big city under Fundadome is looking like Anycity now. The only difference between urban and suburban life now is that your neighbors are closer.

And your neighbors all look like you. In their rush to clear the way for new tourists and residents-as-tourists, many big American cities have engaged in a kind of benign ethnic cleansing on a level not seen since the urban renewal/removal programs of the mid-twentieth century. Sissies are happy and comfortable only when they're surrounded by other Sissies. As Sissies have plowed back into urban centers, their SUVs and double-wide strollers have shoved everyone else out—the poor, the foreign, the strange, the artsy-fartsy. Cities were once living laboratories where the American experiment in democracy was conducted and American culture was created. They're not creating much anymore, just recreating.

Mentioning the postmodern philosopher Jean Baudrillard at this juncture is, how you Frenchies say, *de rigueur*. Because Baudrillard saw this coming thirty-odd years ago. Back when Fundadome was still under construction. He was morbidly fascinated by what the "deep-frozen infantile world" of Disneyland really said about America. Disneyland, he decided, "is there to conceal the fact that it is…all of 'real' America, which is Disneyland… Disneyland is presented as imaginary…when in fact all of Los Angeles and the America surrounding it are no longer real…"

The Matrix borrowed heavily from Baudrillard's idea that the postmodern world was a simulation of reality, but he was not much impressed with the film. It depressed him that people who really do live in a simulated world would sit in movie theaters being entertained by a blockbuster movie about a fictional simulated world. It was like Disneyland squared. He felt it lied to its audience by suggesting that the simulated world was a fantasy, safely enclosed within the confines of the sci-fi genre and the movie theater, when in fact the real Matrix was everywhere around them when they stepped *out* of the movie theater.

A lot of people think Baudrillard was wacky, and in fact, like many other postmodern scholars, he often disappeared up his own butt as he pursued his theories to ridiculous extremes. But he was certainly on the right track about the disneyfication of life under Fundadome.

Jane Jacobs, the urban antiplanner who fought throughout the second half of the twentieth century to save us from the one-city-fits-all schemes of the technorati, also saw this coming. In the early '60s she warned: "There is a quality even meaner than outright ugliness or disorder, and this meaner quality is the dishonest mask of pretended order, achieved by ignoring or suppressing the real order that is struggling to exist and be served."

Forty-odd years later, there doesn't seem to be much struggle left in us. Sure, we do feel some twitches of atavistic yearning or just plain nostalgia for reality. "Adventure tourism" is a thriving niche market. Instead of a completely predictable, prepackaged vacation at Sandals or on a cruise ship, some Sissies court the possibility of the unexpected and a soupçon of danger on packaged tours of more exotic locales—mountaineering, spelunking, treks through jungles or deserts. It's a far cry from the actual adventures and dangers our forefathers faced exploring such places, but at least you get some exercise.

Big-game safari parks offer Sissies a quick and easy simulation of the thrill of the hunt. It's the functional equivalent of going fishing by dropping a hand grenade into a barrel of fish. When Vice President Dick Cheney shot his companion in the face while quail hunting, the mortifying truth was that the quail weren't wild quail and the hunters weren't really hunting. The birds had been farm-bred. They possessed all the survival instincts of your average toy poodle. They were hauled out to the bushes in nets, while the "hunters" were hauled out there in vehicles. No boring, time-consuming stalking was involved. The hunters were shown where to line up, the birds were released, and a moment of well-planned mayhem ensued. The remarkable thing is that Mr. Cheney was such a bad shot that he managed to screw up even under these conditions.

This kind of simulated hunting is widely available inside Fundadome. You can go on a three-hour "safari" to "hunt" farm-raised "wild" boar, deer, antelope and more "exotic" species in complete safety and comfort, and with the money-back guarantee that you *will* bag a trophy.

In 2005, an entrepreneurial soul in Texas took the idea to its logical next step: Internet hunting. At Live-Shot.com, you could sit at your home computer, use your mouse to put the crosshairs on a farm-raised boar wandering innocently up to a food station, and click, triggering an actual shot from an actual on-site gun. Your "trophy" was bagged and delivered to you, just as though you'd called Domino's and ordered a wild boar pizza.

Sissies raised an uproar, many states banned the practice, and Live-Shot.com stopped offering it. But you have to admit that in its horrible way it was kind of brilliant. Why was it seen as so much more offensive than Cheney-style hunting? Internet hunting was no more cynical; it was practically indistinguishable from the galaxy of shooting games Sissies play every day, and at least no friendster in your online hunting party caught a faceful of buckshot.

But never mind. The Japanese are making great strides in robotics, and *Westworld*-like theme parks where you can hunt anything from a fake Tyrannosaurus to animatronic Islamoterrorists will surely open tomorrow.

So here we are, our empire teetering on the brink of collapse into utter Sissitude and downright silliness, and some of us are only just getting hip to the fact that we even have an empire. Until pretty recently, the only Americans who admitted that the American empire existed were the bullsheviks, the peaceniks, the Chomsky-parroting subscribers to *The Nation*. Everyone else was offended by the very idea.

"What, *us* an empire? Are you joking? Didn't we create ourselves struggling *against* imperialist colonialism? Aren't we the world's shining City on the Hill, its beacon of democracy and freedom? The nicest guys on the planet? Aren't we all the time freeing weaker peoples from evil empires? Golly, we would never, *ever* be an imperialist colonial power!"

In one way this was true. After colonizing a large portion of the North American continent—which we told ourselves was nation building, not colonialism—Americans made only a limp, Johnny-Appleseed-come-lately gesture toward the game of global Monopoly the Brits and Europeans and Turks and Russians all played. We took the Philippines, Hawaii, Guam, and some other little islands, messed around with Cuba and Japan and Panama, and that was about it. Our hearts just weren't into building an empire that old-school way.

Instead, we built our empire the American way, the nice-guy way. We became proxy imperialists. We built our empire on money and pop culture and on "extending," rather than openly imposing, our power. Instead of colonizing other nations outright, we left them standing as superficially sovereign entities but dominated them politically and economically. We used our burgeoning military might not to crush other nations, but to free them from evil empires like the Nazis and Japs and Soviets, after which they became our "clients" and "allies" (as did the Germans and Japs and Rooskies, the blood still dripping from their noses). We signed treaties and trade agreements with these nations, built them new cities and factories, stationed our troops on their soil "for their protection," sent them *Star Wars* and Madonna and Coke and McDonald's and Google and blue jeans and Kools and s'mores and Jesus. We offered to sell them space under Fundadome. We held the mortgages and set the interest rates.

When the Soviet empire crumbled and Americans found themselves the last superpower standing, it became harder to deny that the American empire not only existed, it *fuckin' rooled, man.* The bullsheviks kept moaning and maundering about it, while the neocons and patriots started doing the alpha-chimp end-of-history victory dance.

There's another way the American empire differs from the traditional version. When you look at history—sorry, I meant the History Channel—most of the great superpower empires of the past seem to have gone through three distinct phases, over long periods of time. Imperial China, the Romans, the Ottomans, the Brits all did it this way:

- the aggressive, expansionist empire-building phase
- the superpower phase, when the empire is up and humming and nothing much changes for some long period of stability
- the gradual decline and fall

Sissy Nation seems to have compressed the second and third phases into one. By the time we even realized we had an empire up and running, Fundadome was sheltering us and we were well into our decadent, Sissified late-empire phase.

Well, we always were a giddy-up culture.

From the outside, Fundadome is transparent. The whole rest of the world stares at us through it. Some with envy, some with longing, some with admiration, some with fear, some with unconcealed disgust, some with bemused condescension.

Inside, the walls of Fundadome are nearly opaque, dark and smoky gray like the windows on a stretch limo. We can barely see the rest of the world through our own reflection. With all the information in the world at our fingertips, most of us Stoopits remain abysmally ignorant about the world.

This is why when we venture out Beyond Fundadome we so often blunder around like big, dumb Baby Hueys. Whether we go out there as tourists or soldiers or corporate emissaries or missionaries, we're completely unprepared for life Beyond Fundadome and we're astounded to find it's, you know, different. We're flummoxed when someone Beyond Fundadome doesn't talk like us, think like us, act like us, eat like us, pray like us, want what we want, want what we have, want what we offer.

I once sat in the breakfast room of a very nice little hotel in Paris and listened to an American Sissy whine and bluster at the waitress because they didn't have his particular brand of decaf breakfast tea. *Decaf breakfast tea. In Paris.* She had brought him wonderful café au lait and croissants and pastries and fruit, but he had to have his decaf breakfast tea. He was outraged. He pouted and harrumphed and snorted. The success of his whole trip was hanging from that teabag string. The girl was North African and evidently didn't know much English, so he did that dumbass thing of demanding his teabag LOUDER and *LOUDER*, as though the meaning might eventually penetrate her thick foreigner's skull.

I wanted to push his butter knife through his neck. I would have been doing us all a favor.

I've seen a thousand examples of that kind of Stoopit's European Vacation scene, and so have you. Americans—and Brits and Germans—working themselves into self-righteous snits because they can't find the brand of beer they drink at home, or the phones work differently, or the restaurant doesn't have lo-fat oleomargarine, and no one seems to know the score of last's night's Red Sox game—or care! What are these people, barbarians?

There's an American-style bar in the heart of lovely, historical Rome. It serves Budweiser and shows baseball and football on TV. It has been packed with Americans every time I've walked past it.

Why do you leave home at all?

And that's just Paris and Rome. There are a lot of foreign places that are tremendously more foreign.

Obviously this sort of ignorance extends to our foreign policy, our business ventures, our do-gooder charities and missionary operations. We may not be a traditional colonial superpower, but we galumph around the world displaying a traditional paternalism and condescension, trooping through other people's cultures like we're liberating Sicily all over again, patting everyone on the head and handing out Hershey bars.

But not everyone is so glad to see us anymore, and that shocks us and hurts our feelings. In the old days, when we liberated you from an evil empire you ran to cheer us in the streets, toss flowers at us, give us your daughters. Nowadays the response is more like, "Yeah, um, thanks. We'll take it from here. If Saddam comes back we may call you."

We offer to bring you American-style democracy as easily as a KFC American-style fried-chicken franchise, and you're like, "Thanks, but it's not really to our taste. Our diet leans more toward despotic strongman leadership based on our long tradition of tribal conflict. We'll taste a bit of this democracy thing to be polite, but we probably won't like it."

We come to your Dark Continent, the Thirdest World, bring-ing you Christianity and condoms and downmarket drugs *for your own good*, and you have the temerity to shrug and say, "Look, we appreciate the gesture, but we have our traditional ways of doing things. Plus we don't quite trust your GlaxoSmithKline. No offense."

Liberal Sissies wring their hands all the time over how the rest of the world sees us. Others of us don't really care. Why be concerned that the French don't like us? The French don't even like the French. And they're Sissies, too. Hell, the French sort of invented Sissiness, and the language and tude to go with it.

The Swedes, the Brits, and all the rest of western Europe are Sissies as well. There was a beautiful demonstration of Brit Sissi-tude in 2007, and it happened, in fact, in Rome. An army of Brit-ish soccer hooligans descended on the city, spent the pregame hours getting drunk, as is their habit, and later got unruly and violent, which they seem to take as their birthright. The Rome police beat the hell out of them, as was their privilege. For the next several days, battered, hungover soccer hooligans were all over the international media, whining about "brutality" and "use of excessive force" and *threatening to sue*. You couldn't ask for a more perfect demonstration of the hypermasculine bully-boy as a Sissy in drag.

So if it's important for Brit Sissies' and Eurosissies' self-esteem to act condescending toward us now that we've got an empire and they don't, what the hell.

Then there are all the world's Non-Sissies—or, more accu-rately, Not Yet Sissies. Ongoing terrorist activities, the resistance to Pax Americana in places like Iraq and Afghanistan, our on-again off-again relations with China and Pakistan and various other East and South Asian cultures, the persistence of South American fauxialists like Chávez ranting old-school anti-Ameri-canisms…they all demonstrate that we probably *do* need to care about their opinions of us. If only as a matter of self-interest and self-preservation.

Previously, the major global conflicts have been framed as clashes of empires, clashes of cultures, clashes of nation-states, East versus West, North versus South, industrial versus preindustrial, capitalism versus communism, democracy versus fascism, Christianity versus Islam.

All obsolete.

It's time for a new paradigm.

**The world is now divided into
Sissy Nations and Not Yet Sissy Nations.**

The Sissy Nations correspond more or less to what are called the developed nations. The nucleus are the ones who send their Sissy leaders to those Sissy G8 summits: the United States, UK, Russia, Japan, France, Germany, Canada (for organizing the committees and issuing the white papers, the kind of bureaucratic paper pushing Canadians love to do), and Italy (for the catering). Together, they run roughly 70 percent of the world's economy. They have their summits mainly as the only way they can think of to get their Sissy young people out of Starbucks for some fresh air and good old-fashioned youthful fun at their Sissy I-hate-my-daddy protests.

Toss in the rest of western Europe. Leave out Australia. Australia might be the one developed nation that belongs over in the Not Yet Sissy column, or at least is Not Very Sissy. Yet. Then again, as one place where people still seem to unreservedly like and admire Americans, it probably won't be long before Australians fully embrace their own Sissitude.

The rest of the world's nations and cultures are in various stages of Not Yet Sissitude. Being Not Yet Sissies, they're not as genericized and homogenized as Sissies. But clearly, behind all the differences of politics and cultures and religions and traditions and levels of development, many Not Yet Sissies would *love* to be in a position to Sissify themselves. Many of the grievances and much of the conflict in the world come down to that old wanna-banana question, "Hey, how come *they* get to be Sissies and we don't?"

How the Sissies respond to this question may be the key to world peace and prosperity in the coming decades. Continuing the old colonialist program of either exploiting or ignoring the rest of the world will only perpetuate the grievances and strife. The Sissies must encourage the Not Yet Sissies, help them along, and expand Fundadome until it covers all of World World.

How hard would it be? Latin America is already halfway Sissy and would progress a lot quicker if the Latin American elites were convinced to stop hogging all the power, wealth, and Sissiness. Demographically and culturally, North America is being inexorably absorbed into Latin America anyway. The trick would be a simple swap, a two-way flow of influences: as all of the Americas become one big Latin America, it could also all be Sissified.

Sub-Saharan Africa is already on the way to becoming a giant theme park, Africa World Safari Park. That project needs to be completed. Thousands of miles of shoreline wait to be transformed into Seafariland resorts and Seizure World beachfront retirement communities. Kilimanjaro cries out for its Alpine Village ski lodges, Congo awaits its Jungle Gym Fitness Centers, the Serengeti needs just a light dusting of Disney to become the Dark Continent Adventure Park & Big Games Family Fun Center.

Themeparking the continent into a new Africamericaland will suit the world's Sissies, but what to do with the indigenous population? In colonialist days we might have simply displaced or exterminated them, but that sort of brutality is not the Sissy way. The people of Africa need to be equal partners in the Sissifying of their lands. There's more than enough to go around. There are acres of diamonds there.

China is a question. It has the world's largest population and the fourth-largest economy and is well down the path to becoming a superpower, but going about it in its own way, as it has for millennia. China must be discouraged from becoming an obstinate Non-Sissy superpower, maintaining old global rifts and tensions. That's so twentieth century. The Rooskies got with the program, and so should the Chinese.

India's got the second-largest population and they are *so* ready to be Sissified that it should be a piece of cake.

Current appearances notwithstanding, the Islamic world is *way* Sissy already. Count the ways:

Muslims are often knee-jerk fundamentalists, just like American Sissies.

Many Muslims are even touchier and more easily offended than American Sissies. American Sissies can't take a joke; Muslim Sissies can't even take a cartoon.

Muslim fundamentalist men are terrified of their women. American Sissy males try to hide from their women; Muslim Sissy males try to hide their women. They cover them up in burkas and make believe they're not there.

Suicidal terrorism is how war is waged by Sissies too stoopit and self-segregated into victim identity groups to get organized in proper military fashion. Look up the Six-Day War, the Arab Vietnam. They threw all their armies against tiny Israel and got their faces kicked. Arab manhood has never recovered.

They're totally into virtual reality. There are more Muslim terrorist sites on the Web than there are porn sites.

They're often craven label whores, mad fashionistas, and as gadget-crazed as any American Sissy.

They may be the world's most complete victim/bully culture. How did some Muslims respond when the pope "victimized" them by calling them a violent culture? They went on a violent rampage, destroying property, killing a nun, and threatening holy war.

Really, the so-called clash of Islam versus the West is just a tiff between two variations of Sissy fundamentalism, which could be easily resolved if both sides would simply agree that they have more in common than in conflict, both being knockoffs of Judaism.

Think about how much nicer it will be—for *all* of us—when the world is completely Sissified, safe and clean and comfortable and familiar and genericized, every one of us surrounded by our toys and gadgets and dripping with bling, never threatened by sharp edges or slippery surfaces or the unfamiliar or foreign, plugged into virtuality 24/7, our ears stoppered and our eyes glued to the screen, dealing with one another only through text messages and MySpace. All living under one great Fundadome, and all of us getting along because each of us is alone in his/her own private little bubble anyway.

This future is within our grasp. Only our Sissy fatalism, laziness, and stoopitness hold us back.

Sissy: "Wait wait wait. That's all you've got to say about that? What's your *plan* for Sissifying the world, smart guy?"

Me: All I'm saying is the world is crowded with Not Yet Sissies who'd love the opportunity to become fat, lazy, decadent Sissies like us. Either we give them the opportunity, or they're going to come eat us. Don't ask me to hand you a ten-point master plan for how to do it. Use your own brains for once and work something out.

What? You don't think we can pull that off? Sissy.

Or is it that you don't think we *should* pull it off?

Why is that? Could it be that, despite living the safest, healthiest, longest, best-fed, most coddled, most entertained, most comfortable lives of any humans ever, we Sissies are still not happy? That instead of enjoying our exceptional good fortune, we're a bunch of whiny, lazy, fat, soft, stoopit, fearful, carping babies? Or brutally ignorant, resentful, sullen, hypersexual, attention-and-respect-demanding bully babies? And we're just smart enough to know that we'd hate a world filled with people like us?

There's a great *Twilight Zone* episode that addresses exactly this dilemma. Shelley Berman plays the quintessential American Sissy—a nasty, complaining, narcissistic, solipsistic, touchy bastard who thinks he's superior to everyone and moans and sighs and tsk-tsks, "People people people people." He wishes he were alone in the world, and he gets his wish. Then he gets lonely and wishes the world were populated again, only with people just like him. He gets his wish again—a whole world full of identical, nasty, complaining, narcissistic Shelley Berman Sissies.

It aired in 1961, another example of sci-fi doing a pretty fine job of looking ahead and seeing…us.

Then again, we knew before the 1960s that there would be a price to pay for all our safety and sameness and knee-jerk conformity.

Part of that price is the yawning boredom that we try to fend off by filling every second of our lives with more and more entertainments and useless trivia and inane text-chatter and gadgets and being busy looking busy.

Part of it is the loneliness, disconnectedness, and callous disregard that come from having insulated and isolated ourselves from the world and from each other.

Part of it is derived from the nagging realization that we've lost our individuality and independence. Look at how nobody really has a life anymore, just a *lifestyle*. Jesus, what a repulsive word, but what a fittingly genericized, consumerist term for the prepackaged, off-the-rack Sissy simulation of life. We sense the loss of ourselves, and try to re-create a personality through narcissism and victim identity politics and public confession and celebrity fantasies. But none of that quite adds up to a living, breathing human being with a sense of self, a sense of accomplishment, and, most important, a sense of purpose.

Part of it is the constant fear and anxiety that come from having relinquished all responsibility for our own lives to the boss and the experts and the government. The less we feel in control of our lives and well-being, the more easily spooked we are. We're children, looking to the government as to a parent who'll shelter us and tell us what to do. We're more willing to give up rights and let the government and experts intrude into our personal lives in exchange for being protected from the big, bad world. They become the enablers of our childish fears.

Ignorance figures in here as well. Ignorance isn't bliss, it's paranoia. When you're a little kid you're scared of the dark, of what's in the closet or under your bed. As you get older and wiser those fears vanish. Primitive cultures are rife with childish superstitions. The more you know about the world and how things work, the less anxious it all makes you.

But we Sissies don't grow older and wiser. We just become bigger babies. Infants for life. Frightened, demanding, resentful, self-absorbed, passive-aggressive Sissy-bullies.

Finally, a big part of the price we pay is not knowing that *there's a difference between a fulfilled life and a life—sorry, I meant lifestyle— merely filled with junk.* We have dead-end jobs and dead-end lives and dead-end families and know we're not happy but we don't know why. We think that if we keep loyally consuming more and more crap it'll somehow make us happy. Like hogs in pens, we consume consume consume, mindlessly, relentlessly, and joylessly. We eat to grotesque obesity, or buy the biggest, loudest plasma TV on the block, or the newest zillion-function cell phone, or the most godzilloid SUV, or wear tons of bling, or live in gigantic McMansions…and somehow none of it makes us happy, *because none of it changes who we are.* No matter how wide your TV screen is, you're still the same fat slob sprawled there staring at it. No matter how big your SUV is, you still drive it to the same screamingly dull job to make the payments on it.

You can't whine, wish, or buy your way to "happiness," whatever that is. We all know this in our hearts, we've been told it a million times, but we ignore it. If God exists, he's not our slave, and the Universe for sure isn't a giant mail-order catalogue. It's craven Sissitude to simply expect and demand to be *made* happy, then get all mopey and reach for the corn chips or Zoloft when God or the Universe disappoints you again.

Whatever happiness is, it's clearly something we have to achieve. We have to *do* something that makes us feel good about ourselves, useful, productive. That may not be your job. In corporate consumerist Sissy Nation, lots of us—probably most of us—have jobs that aren't exactly "fulfilling." They're more about us simply filling space and filling time. So maybe it's raising a family, or getting involved in something extracurricular that you feel strongly about, or cultivating a talent that's never going to help you pay the bills. But whatever the happy life is, it isn't a passive or passive-aggressive one. Filling your gut and your home and your life with junk is not fulfillment. Lying around wishing you were happy and resenting other people's happiness is Sissy. Whining that the world won't *let* you be happy is *totally* Sissy.

The fact that we have become a Sissy Nation does not mean that we are all—uniformly and thoroughly and equally—stoopitized and Sissified individuals. Lots of folks are religious but not fundamentalist. Some still know the difference between an ethical choice and blind obedience to an arbitrary rule. Some still know how to hold a political, social, or moral point of view without going all knee-jerk and sanctimonious about it. Some still act out a pioneering, adventurous, innovative spirit. A few folks still seem to know the difference between reality and reality TV. A few still think for themselves.

Some still get off their butts and *act* on their principles, trying to make a personal difference and *change* what they don't like rather than just whine about it. You may not always agree with the change they're trying to bring about—pro-choice, anti-immigration, whatever it is—but at least they're doing something. One easy example: Geoffrey Canada, a guy born poor and black in the South Bronx, who created the Harlem Children's Zone, an attempt to foster a *real* community and a *real* social network in a setting where those things are *real* hard to come by. Definitely not a Sissy. Look him up—he's gotten lots of press. Oprah is a fan. Oprah herself vacillates between promoting quintessential Sissiness like *The Secret* one day and then anti-Sissiness like the

Harlem Children's Zone or her own Oprah Winfrey Leadership Academy for Girls the next.

Lance Armstrong sure don't look like a Sissy. Not to mention having the best American hero name of any person alive today. The Williams sisters ain't Sissies. Schwarzenegger seems to have done a decent job of resisting Sissitude, despite being Governator of a very Sissy state. It's got nothing to do with his hypermasculine bulk and all his girly-man riffing. It's about his apparently having some clear opinions, values, and convictions, and being willing to act on them.

You can maybe name some more of these people. You may even claim to be one yourself. You've read a book. That's a hopeful sign.

But hopeful signs and all-star exceptions to the rule are only so useful. As a group, as a society, as a culture, we have *undeniably* been stoopitized and Sissified. We all swim in this Sissy Sea. As the Gore-huggers among us are fond of pointing out, no creature is unaffected by its ecosystem. Sissiness is our social ecosystem, and most of us have absorbed at least some Sissitude. The war for Oprah's Sissy soul is a good illustration. You may be a manly-man cowboy or fireman or karate expert, but if you're also a knee-jerk conformist label whore about your politics or your clothes or social views, you've got some Sissy in you. You can be the ballsiest bulldyke on the planet, but if you're also a mindlocked PC fundamentalist about whatever beliefs you hold, that's your Sissy showing. You may be hell in the office or on the trading floor, but if you look, think, talk, and act exactly like everyone else in your yuppie cohort, you're a Sissy. If you're basically an upstanding citizen and parent but also overprotecting and overfeeding and overmedicating your kids, that's you expressing your inner Sissy through them. If you work at having people think you're the bangingest gangsta or hippest hipster in the hood, that's your Sissitude.

Okay, we're coming to the wrap-up here. Let's take a few last calls.

Sissy: "You're just a cynic."

Me: Classic. Sissies are all the time mistaking criticism for cynicism. A true cynic wouldn't bother. He'd figure it's hopeless. Sissies are so used to having our truth edited, soft-focused, and sugar-coated for us, so touchy, so trained in the hypocritical politeness of PC prevarication, so terrified of any word or thought that might be labeled offensive, that harsh truths and cold realities are dismissed as cynicism. Incapable of analytical or critical thinking, Sissies can only complain. Complaining is okay. Complaining we're used to. It comes packaged with our victim lifestyles. But don't be critical. If you don't have anything good to say about us, just shut the hell up.

Sissy: "Why are you so negative? What you call the Sissy Age I see as a time of real social and technological progress."

Me: True, not *everything* that's happened in the past fifty years has been negative. As noted earlier, the civil rights movement, which got under way at the dawn of the Sissy Age, was a great thing—*until* we Sissified and stoopitized it into its whiny stepchild, the victim identity group movement. Still, we did become marginally more respectful of and sensitive about (oh, are we *sensitive*) all those "differences" of culture and sexuality and what have you that coexist under Fundadome. It's surely a better time to be, for instance, gay or black. You can certainly get around easier in a wheelchair. And so on. *Not that anyone stopped whining about it all.*

And yes, the personal computer and the Internet and cable TV and the hydrogen car and lung transplants are all wonderful, okay? Maybe someday we might even figure out how to use it all to make us *less* stoopit and Sissy instead of more.

See? What's cynical about that? Next caller please.

Sissy: "None of this is new. I've been hearing it all my life."

Me: That's absolutely correct. Forster saw the Age of the Sissy coming a hundred years ago, Whyte documented its early stages fifty years ago, young people kinda-sorta rebelled against it forty years ago, Baudrillard noodled about it thirty years ago, and today we all know, or at least sense, that we're living in it. But it's gotten awfully end-of-empire and *I, Claudius* around here, folks, and if ever there was a time when the restatement of the obvious was the first duty of intelligent men—oh all right, *persons*—it's now.

Sissy: "It's easy to be critical. What do you propose we *do* about all this?"

Me: We've been hearing answers to that all our lives, too. We just haven't lifted a finger to act on them.

To start with, *maybe we should be grateful to live in conditions where we have the luxury even to think about living "a fulfilled life,"* when so many people in the world have to focus all their efforts on staying alive, period. We're the luckiest humans who ever drew breath. Maybe we should be doing more with that air than just whining and carping and blabbing endlessly about ourselves on our cells. Maybe we should be taking advantage of our unique and privileged situation to do something *useful*, instead of just growing fatter, softer, lazier, more fearful, disengaged, selfish, Stoopit, and Sissy.

Some of the steps toward de-Stoopitizing and de-Sissifying ourselves probably include:

* Stop your whining.
* Stop thinking of yourselves as victims.
* Stop blaming others for your own faults, your weaknesses, your disappointments, your failures, your discontent.
* Stop looking to God, the universe, the lottery, the fridge, and the medicine cabinet for quick-and-easy happiness.
* Stop confusing fundamentalism for conviction and knee-jerk obedience to arbitrary rules for ethical behavior.

- Stop celebrating false pride and demanding unearned respect. *Do* something to be proud of and *earn* respect.
- Stop confusing a fulfilling life with a life that's just filled with crap.
- Stop fearing and hiding from reality.
- Start using your brain and thinking for yourself. That's why God gave it all those extra wrinkles.
- Get off your ass. Get active in your own life and engaged in the world. Make yourself useful around here, instead of just taking up space in front of the TV.

You should probably not try to de-Sissify yourself in one great leap. You'd only disappoint yourself and start whining for someone to come along and do it for you. Maybe start with small, easy steps. Eat one less handful of pork rinds a day. Watch thirty minutes of BBC News instead of ECW tonight. Start walking to the second floor instead of taking the elevator. Take 10 percent of the pay you usually drop on the lottery every week and put it in the bank. Whatever.

Sissy: "Be disciplined, watch less TV, don't eat too much, be an individual. Who can argue with that? What are you saying now that my mother didn't teach me when I was seven?"

Me: The American Sissy is now the fattest and laziest humanoid who ever lay around the planet, the stoopitest person in the industrialized world, and the most knee-jerk fundamentalist outside the Taliban. Obviously you weren't listening to your mother. You're breaking her heart. She asked me to try this last-ditch intervention.

But I'm not your mother, and this *sure* isn't *The Secret*, or any other self-help book for you to buy and ignore. You know the answers. We all do. Whether or not you lift a finger to act on them is up to you, Sissy.

Sissy: "Would any of those steps make us happier?"

Me: No, not if you mean the mindless contentment of Holsteins.

It would make us *less* Holstein, more human. More freethinking individuals, less groupthinking lemmings. Yes, as the clones in *Body Snatchers* said, it's harder to be a thinking individual than a groupthinking clone. But then, the clones in *Body Snatchers* were Weeds from Outer Space.

I mean, what are our alternatives here? I can think of a few.

We can do that thing of Sissifying the whole world.

Or we can just keep growing fatter and stoopiter here inside Fundadome, ignoring the rest of the world, until some lean and hungry Not Yet Sissy barbarians from Beyond Fundadome come pouring in, jabbing our fat, soft bellies with their bayonets and slurping us down like human oysters.

Or maybe we'll just keep devolving and puddling and slide down the drain without anyone's help. Sink under our own weight. Just...simply...disappear.

That's more or less how Tocqueville envisioned it:

"Because the civilization of ancient Rome perished in consequence of the invasion of the barbarians, we are perhaps too apt to think that civilization cannot perish in any other manner. *If the light by which we are guided is ever extinguished, it will dwindle by degrees, and expire of itself.*" (My emphasis.)

That light has definitely dwindled.

Can we rekindle it? Enter a new post-Sissy age, where we regain our confidence in ourselves and the rightness of what we're doing here, get active and clever and innovative, get engaged in the real world again instead of absorbed in fantasy, face our problems and lick 'em, get back to the moon fer chrissakes and on to Mars and the stars?

A cynic would say no, of course not, we're too fat and lazy and stoopit and Sissy. Game over, man. Game over.

What do you say, Sissy?

If a branch of a tree is
frozen into a pond, you cannot
pull it out without breaking off
the sealed in end. If multiple
ends are sealed in at
different points, then the best
way to remove it is to wait
for the pond to melt,
Or to melt it yourself,

REFERENCES

I take sole responsibility for the opinions in this book. But I did borrow some facts, ideas, and quotations from others.

The Orwell quote that opens this book is from his magnificent *Essays* (Alfred A. Knopf, 2002).

The bit about fatalistic politicians offering us glum choices (page 9) comes from Frank Furedi's excellent *Politics of Fear* (Continuum, 2005). I refer to this book again on page 93.

The *New England Journal of Medicine* study (page 16), "The Spread of Obesity in a Large Social Network over 32 Years," was published in volume 357:370–379, July 26, 2007. It's online at http://content.nejm.org/cgi/content/full/357/4/370. The Saletan article in *Slate* is at http://www.slate.com/id/2171214/fr/flyout.

My thoughts about AIDS fundamentalism (page 24) have been much influenced by Celia Farber's reporting over the years, some of it collected in her book *Serious Adverse Events* (Melville House, 2006).

William H. Whyte Jr.'s *The Organization Man* (page 32) was published by Simon & Schuster in 1956.

The *New York* article about grups (page 41) is Adam Sternbergh's "Up with Grups," in the April 3, 2006, issue.

To see some of the Pentagon's nonlethal weaponry (page 71) in action, check out its Web site, https://www.jnlwp.com/Default.asp.

"A Sisterhood of Grief," by Edward L. Linenthal (page 74), ran in the *New York Times* on December 23, 2001.

My discussion of maunfactured disease panics that begins on page 80 borrows a lot from Marc Siegel's *False Alarm* (Wiley, 2006).

The *New York Times* article about Project BioShield (page 83), Eric Lipton's "U.S. Cancels Order for 75 Million Doses of Anthrax Vaccine," ran on December 20, 2006.

James M. Glass's *"Life Unworthy of Life"* (page 85) was published by Basic Books in 1997.

The information on Swedish and Danish sissies (page 94) came from the article "Swedes as 'Safety Junkies,' " by Ivar Ekman in the *International Herald Tribune,* January 4, 2006.

The Secret (page 98), by Rhonda Byrne, was published by Atria Books in 2006.

Karen A. Cerulo's *Never Saw It Coming* (page 100) was published by the University of Chicago Press in 2006.

Irving L. Janis's *Victims of Groupthink* (page 101) was published by Houghton Mifflin in 1972.

The quotes from Benjamin Franklin and John Adams about equality (pages 109–10) I copped from a 1961 essay by R. Carter Pittman, "Equality Versus Liberty," which I read online at http://rcarterpittman.org/essays/misc/Equality_v_Liberty.html.

The Tocqueville citations on page 110 and elsewhere are from the Bantam paperback edition of *Democracy in America* (2002).

Vonnegut's "Harrison Bergeron" (page 110) is in the collection *Welcome to the Monkey House* (Dial Press, 1968).

Christopher Lasch's *The Culture of Narcissism* (page 115) was published by W. W. Norton in 1978.

For in-depth coverage of campus speech codes and other politically correct tramplings of students' rights (page 124), consult the Foundation for Individual Rights in Education at www.thefire.org.

Thomas McEvilley's *Art & Discontent* (page 133) was published by McPherson & Company in 1991.

E. M. Forster's "The Machine Stops" (page 140) is in *The Machine Stops and Other Stories* (Andre Deutsch, 1998).

The Jean Baudrillard quote on page 145 is from *Simulations*, published by Semiotext(e) in 1983.

The Jane Jacobs quote on page 146 is from *The Death and Life of Great American Cities*, republished by Random House in 2002.

25 - *Ubi dubium ibi libertas*

ACKNOWLEDGMENTS

As usual, I exploited the smarts, patience, and resources of several friends, colleagues, and loved ones as I was thinking about and writing this book. I am deeply indebted to Brian Berger, Lauri Bortz, William Bryk, Justice Buckmaster, Richard Byrne, Chris Calhoun, Carole Carroll, Celia Farber, Keach Hagey, Mimi Kramer, Rasha Refaie, Ken Swezey, Kurt Thometz, Tony Trachta, and Christine Walker.

Many thanks to Mr. Ken Siman, publisher of Virgin Books USA, and all his staff, for being so Non-Sissy. And to Laura Lindgren for her great cover and layout, and to Anna Jardine and Don Kennison for their astute copyediting and proofreading.